Dr. Ni

Damaged, bu
Now What!

MW01289993

Publishing Consultant
The Pierce Agency, LLC
www.ThePierceAgencyLLC.com

Cover Design
Sassi Concepts & Designs, Inc.

Printed in the U.S.A.
ISBN -13: 978-1537242033
ISBN -10: 1537242032

To schedule an interview with Dr. Garris-Watson, or to book for a speaking engagement, email an inquiry to booking@wodwm.org. For reprint permission, or to use text or graphics from this publication, e-mail your request to DamagedButDestined@gmail.com.

DEDICATION

This book is dedicated to those who have endured the damage of life that others would use to deem you as destroyed, but that God instead is using to shape your destiny. It has happened, but it does not have permission to hold you hostage. Likewise, this book is also dedicated to my foster grandmother, Florence Greene, who first and consistently showed me the love of God, and to my children, Steven, II and Sasha, the best parts of me.

ACKNOWLEDGEMENTS

To God who is the source of everything that I am. It takes a great God to use my story for His glory. To the "answer to my prayers wrapped in flesh," my husband, Bishop James E. Watson, thank you for being the conduit of God's love towards me. You have taught me what it feels like to be protected. I honor you for being strong enough to allow me to be both strong and soft simultaneously. You are indeed the epitome of a Strong Man!

To my Man-child and Princess – Steven and Sasha – thank you for all that you represent to me. I am convinced that God gave me both of you to help me understand the depths of His love for me. The fruit of my womb is indeed blessed. Thank you for unselfishly sharing me to do ministry.

To my anointed sister (times 3) and Executive Assistant, Prophet Sachiko Goode, your unwavering belief in me and this book have been the motivation on the most difficult days. When I think of family, I think of you.

Prophetess Thomosa Dixon, my "SisterFriend," daily I give thanks to God for you in my prayers. True friends are a gift from God that we have the privilege to unwrap daily. To my high school classmate and workplace pastor, Dr. Darius Beechaum, thank you for pushing me into my doctoral destiny.

Rebekah L. Pierce and The Pierce Agency, your service was a God-send providing the divine push that I needed to bear down and give birth to this book. I am praying that doors will swing open for the world to have access to the great work that you do.

Last, but certainly not least, to all of those who have shared a part in my spiritual journey, whether as a lesson or a blessing, I am grateful for the part that you have played. Apostle Joyce Bailey and the House of Prayer family, thank you for allowing me to have a safe place to cry out to God and learn His purpose for my life. Rev. CC Jackson, Pastor Lisa Veney, Apostle Shirley Johnson and Apostle Henrietta Brooks, thank you for being vessels for God's use as He strategically placed you in my life while I transitioned into and continue to grow in ministry. To the many other leaders and ministers of the gospel that I have learned from whether through observation, information, evaluation or impartation, God bless you as you have me. Extra special love to my Words of Deliverance Worldwide Ministries (www.WODWM.org) family, friends and covenant partners; each of you represents fruit from my fight. I am fully convinced that among your ranks, I am surrounded by greatness.

Dr. Nikita C. Garris-Watson

INTRODUCTION

"Damaged, but Destined"

2 Corinthians 4: 8 we are troubled on every side, yet not distressed; we are perplexed, but not in despair; 9 Persecuted, but not forsaken; cast down, but not destroyed.

The idea was to tell this story chronologically, however, as with life, it didn't turn out that way. There are sections where the story is sequential and moments where the story is grouped by situation or topic. When discussing the healing processes, pieces of the past intermingled with present experiences to shape the format of what is being shared. It is important, however, for those who will read this book to understand that contained within these pages are pieces of my life's story as I lived and remember them. It is not an exhaustive biography, but rather a collection of critical moments that have impacted my on-going faith journey. For years, I tossed and turned with God over the necessity of sharing my life story, especially as I felt that others could do so with greater journalistic proficiency and eloquence. I argued my case before Him many days and nights with a certainty that I would be released from this assignment, but like my Savior in the Garden of Gethsemane, ultimately, my answer would become not *my* will, but *Thy* will be done.

Thus, the sharing of my life is for the sole purpose of bringing God glory while seeking to reach those, who like myself, have withstood the damage that life can bring in various forms. For those who choose to pull back the layers of my life, it is of utmost important that each person understands that my motivation is not to bring shame on others, but rather to illustrate the power of God in even the most difficult of circumstances. It is my sincere prayer that every reader is able to discover the depth of God's love despite the damage that life can and often does inflict.

Which lends itself to the following question: What do you do when you are not created in love, birthed in love or spend a lifetime trying to redefine and understand what it means to be loved? These questions would be part of my life's journey. Molested, abused, abandoned, rejected, depressed, suicidal, self-loathing, promiscuous, hopeless and helpless are just a few of the words that depict the story of much of my existence. Born to a 17 year-old single mother, with no mother, during a time when it was neither popular nor positive, set the stage for a tumultuous life. I would see more than any child should see, hear more than my memory can forget and experience more than my heart could handle on its own.

Warfare would become my way of life and home would be my first battlefield. I would learn the painful lessons of kept secrets and deeply seated hurt. There was never a thought the way was going to get easier for me as I was growing up, for it seemed like the warfare was not going to let up. This story is not one of a fairytale where overnight I would come to live happily ever after. No. This is a story of survival where I learned to appreciate each moment along the way. There are a few "Kingdom Godmothers" who grace these pages and even a "Prince Charming," but he came to help in the fight, not to fix it. As I retrace my life's story, it becomes clearer with each moment that I was born through a fight, to a fight, with a fight and for a fight!

Part I

So What?

Chapter 1 ~ First Memories

"Sometimes you need to stop fighting to stop drowning" (Evy Michaels).

Drowning and the Beating

The event occurred during the summer at a park in Richmond, Virginia. I had to have been no older than eight because my brother was still in his baby carrier. I am able to recall this fact because my mother was sitting on the porch when we returned from the park and he was sitting beside her. I had gone to the park with my mother's best friend, Priscilla, and her daughters. My "Aunt," as I called her, worked for Philip Morris, so I am convinced that this may have been a company picnic because of the amount of people present.

There was a pool at the park, and we were eating at some type of a cookout. I remember getting into the water; I remember playing with the other kids, having a good time, which was a rarity because we didn't get to do a lot as children. Life was always pretty much sad and depressing. I really don't know how it happened, but while in the water, I found myself drowning. One moment I am playing with my "cousins" and the next, I am fighting against the water that is filling my lungs. I don't remember hollering or asking for help. I just remember fighting for air, fighting for my breath. I had learned how to swim when I was three, but somehow, I ended up in the deep end of the pool when we had started in the shallow end. There must have been some sort of transition that put me there.

As I was preparing to succumb to death, the lifeguard snatched me out of the water, laid me on the side of the pool and began pumping my chest to get the excess water out of my body. My Aunt Priscilla came running over frantic because she was scared to death. I could not explain to her or anyone what had happened. When we got back to my brother's grandmother's house, as my mother sat on the porch with my baby brother by her side in the carrier, Aunt Priscilla told my mother what had happened. She didn't blame me for the incident, but she did say quite earnestly, "I can't take you anywhere with me." When I look back on that day, I realize that my aunt said that because she was just scared. I had almost died and she was terrified about what she would have had to tell my mother.

At the time, my expectation was to be embraced for living; after all, I was only eight years-old and had just nearly escaped death, but I was not prepared for what happened next. My mother was dating my brother's father, Jerome, at that time who was extremely abusive to her. I only had a forced relationship with him because I did not trust him. I hated him, in fact, because of his unmerited and unmerciful abuse towards my mother. When we returned to our house, instead of getting a hug or kisses for not dying, surprisingly, I got a beating for nearly drowning. But it wasn't my mother who beat me. She had her abusive boyfriend do it. I had a problem with this because he was *not* my father.

We lived in a two bedroom, one bath apartment with a kitchen and a living room that was sparsely furnished; the place was nothing to really remember. We never had fancy items and I shared a room with my sister who would have been about three years old and my brother as I mentioned earlier who was under a year old. There were two twin beds and a dresser that we all shared. The white toy box was in the bottom of the closet on the left side of the room. There was one window and no curtains. In retrospect, the entire apartment reeked of poverty and depression.

Jerome did not just beat me; he tortured me. He took everything that was in the closet, the drawer and the toy box – toys, books and the few clothes that we had – and dumped them on the floor in my room. He said if I didn't want a beating, I had to get everything up off the floor by the time he came back. It could not have been more than a minute before he returned. I was scrambling to pick everything up, but it was too late. He proceeded to torment me with words – antagonizing me – and then he beat me anyway. He beat me so bad, I bled.

As welts covered my body, I wept in agony; we repeated this routine over and over for about an hour: he'd dump my things, tell me to pick them up and then beat me anyway. I still don't know why my mother felt that allowing him to discipline me was a permissible thing to do. To this day, I can think of nothing that I had done which warranted the response that I had received from nearly drowning. I did not disobey any adults and I did not try to prove that I had any particular skill. It just happened.

I used to question that if the situation had, in fact, required discipline, why didn't my mother do it herself? Why allow a "boyfriend" with whom I had no relationship other than forced interactions to dish out discipline? Likewise, I wondered what lesson was I supposed to have learned from the beating. Our lives at that time was nothing remarkable. So why the beating? What did I miss? What had I done to deserve this?

Dr. Nikita C. Garris-Watson

The Hand of God

"My times are in your hand..." (Psalm 31:5).

When my mother was pregnant with me at age 16 or 17, she was pretty much homeless. Her mother had died when she was 11 years-old. Her father initially abandoned her, but when he learned that she was going to be adopted, he changed his mind about wanting her having discovered that he could get money for her. So he came back and claimed her. Suffering from the loss of her mother at an early age and living with an unaffectionate alcoholic father, my mother really did not have a childhood. It was fraught with heartache and pain, not too dissimilar from what I would experience, ironically.

She would end up eventually with my foster grandmother, Florence Greene, the mother of my mother's high school friend that would be chosen as my godmother, Aunt Sally. I am sure that saying yes to the role, she, too, only seventeen, would have no idea the depth of the coming responsibility. From what I have gathered, my godmother took my mother home with her a few times before she was pregnant, and my mom would just hang around there from time to time because of the family's close relationship and the love they had for one another. So when my mother found out that she was pregnant, Grandma Greene took her in. It is because of this unselfish sacrifice that I hold my grandmother in the highest regard. Although we are not blood related, she has been the one constant in my life. She has been the one that has kept me, that has believed in me and that has always tried to speak life into me. She is who I ended up with when my mother didn't want me and the one that I would run back to many times over the years.

Dr. Nikita C. Garris-Watson

My grandmother taught me faith and the power of prayer. I learned from her how to love beyond what is seen on the surface of a person and believe what I see in the spirit realm regarding the potential of a person. The house where she has lived for over 62 years is the closest representation of home for me. When I think about the special moments in my life, I think about her house. Not because everything was perfect there, but because that was the only place and the family that dwelled there which represented a presence of stability in my early life. Even during the instability that would become my life's story, I knew that she loved me. I lived with her from birth to the age of three and then on again and off again from 13 until into my early adult years. There are only a few times that I ever felt unwanted or unwelcomed at my grandmother's house, but those moments were the result of my troubles becoming too much for anyone to handle. Those moments were few and far between.

My earliest memory of my life is of my grandmother leading me to prayer. I was about two or three years old and we were standing in church. She had on a grey choir robe and she was holding my hand. Her pastor at the time was wearing a white robe with red trim and crosses on it, and I remember him anointing us and her asking him to pray for me. I can clearly see myself in a light blue dress with white socks and shoes looking up with curiosity as his large hand covered my head almost in its entirety. It would be many years before I would spend regular time in church after that day.

Over the years, glimpses of this memory would come to me and I would not fully understand what I was seeing; but one day, in a moment of putting my life into perspective, God allowed me to see this memory uninterrupted for the very first time. I soon realized that with all that I had faced in life – was still facing - that *fleeting* memory would appear every so often to let me know that He had not forsaken me, but that He had His hand on me even when it seemed like it wasn't that way.

Chapter 2 ~ The First Time

"The pain started years ago, but I'd lived with it for so long at that point that I'd accepted it as an inevitable part of me" (Ashley D. Wallis).

My Uncle

My mother is the youngest of five siblings, one sister and three brothers, two which are now deceased. Although I knew all of my mother's siblings, the relationships would vary drastically. I would see my Aunt Mary, who is the oldest of the five siblings, with the greatest frequency. I saw my mother's oldest brother, a truck driver, who was also a constant in my life, and while I loved him sincerely, disagreements with my mother would test this relationship repeatedly as he would make decisions about me based on one-sided untruths. The baby brother, and the one with whom I share a birthday, was in the military, so I would see him intermittently. I did not have much of a relationship with my mother's middle brother, Uncle Leroy, however, only seeing him occasionally.

At the time, I did not find that to be too odd because we did move around a lot, moving from house to house of different family members just to survive. At some point, we did end up living in our own house, and again, I had to share a room with my little sister, but I didn't mind because even as a young child, I felt a strong need to protect my siblings. So the closer she was to me, the better. Soon after we moved into our home, Uncle Leroy came to visit us; that one visit would change my life forever. There'd be no one to protect me.

14

Dr. Nikita C. Garris-Watson

It was the middle of the night and I was in my bed. My younger sister was asleep next to me on my right. I was lying on my back and I felt my uncle come into the room; he came over to my left side and laid down next to me. At first, he just laid there. Then he began to touch me intimately, sexually. I remember being startled and feeling strange. I remember being uncomfortable, but I was not initially scared because I don't think I knew to be scared. I was just so shocked. I remember him whispering, "Just let me put it inside of you."

I didn't even understand what "it" was. And then I felt this piercing pain of being penetrated at six years-old. Not only did my vagina hurt, but my stomach hurt. My chest hurt; my body felt as if it were wrapped in a blanket of pain. I remember not feeling right. And then I was told not to say anything to anybody. "This is our little secret," he said to me. "This is just between you and me. I love you. I wouldn't do anything to hurt you." But he was hurting me. Not only emotionally hurting me, but literally in my body. My little sister was only a little over a year or so old. I remember instinctively wanting to protect her. I knew I didn't want her to hurt, so I did as I was told so as not to wake her up.

It seemed like it took forever for morning to come. The next morning, he reminded me that I was not supposed to tell anybody. "It's our little secret," he said.

I remember my panties were white with flowers on them and had a little purple trim around the band. When I went into the bathroom to clean myself, there was dark red blood caked on the inside of my thighs. I didn't know what to do. When I came out of the bathroom, he was waiting by the door, a physical reminder to not tell anyone what had just happened. I looked for my panties, but I could not find them. I am certain that he took them and threw them away. Now I had no evidence, so to speak, of what had happened to me to even show anybody. So I had a secret and no evidence.

I had always been a quiet child, so I presume that there was not any real outward change in my behavior for anyone to notice after that night. But I knew I was different on the inside. Shortly thereafter, my uncle moved across the country to California. I wouldn't see him again for a few more years. And when I did see him again, I went to great lengths to avoid him. I kept my distance because he was still a touchy-feely person, and he acted as if nothing had happened. That he had not violated a six year-old little girl – his niece. And no one even noticed.

Dr. Nikita C. Garris-Watson

Not Again – My Cousins

Family would be would be the greatest object of my pain. This time while living in a housing project called Fairfield Court in Richmond, Virginia, my older cousin would be the aggressor. I was about seven years-old; it started out with him just touching me, but I felt uncomfortable about it and didn't understand what was really happening. Touching was the result of a game we used to play called 'Hide and Go Seek.' The alternate to that game was 'Hide and Go Get It,' and that's how it started…as a neighborhood game that never was a game.

This "game" would go on for years. He was about five years older than me, so he would be home when I got home from school. If I wanted something to eat, then I would have to do whatever he said. Because we all lived in the same house together, he basically had unlimited access to me. My mother and my aunt worked during the day, so we were often alone. At night, he'd come into the room when the others were asleep (11 of us lived in a two bedroom apartment). I could never say anything because he would warn me not to speak or he'd muffle my mouth with a pillow over my face. The abuse became almost a nasty norm for me until I was about 12 years-old. Even when we didn't live in the same house, it only minimally decreased the frequency of the violations as there were too many other occasions and opportunities for access.

Internally, I was literally shutting down. I was dying on the inside because there were so many other things going on around me that I didn't know what to hurt from. In the midst of this, my mother was in and out of an abusive relationship; we were living in poverty and suffering from the side of effects of living in it. There were so many different challenges occurring all at once it seemed that there was not enough time to hurt from one thing before something else happened. Perhaps the greatest difficulty was that because of what was happening with my mother, I did not dare trust her with my feelings about what I was going through. My thought was that if she couldn't save herself, she surely wouldn't have the strength and courage to save me either. So I remained silent and tormented.

Just when things could not get any more complicated, another cousin began to prey upon me. This time it was my female cousin. We often shared a twin-sized bed because there were not enough beds for everybody. We slept toes to head. She started touching me sexually at the time I was already being molested almost daily by her brother. As with the others, there was no warning. She just started touching me. This happened twice in the middle of the night. I remember the TV being on and the flicker of the light. But as quickly as it started, it ended; unlike what I was enduring at the hands of my male cousin, she just stopped.

She and I would become very close later in life so much so that one day, as I talked with her about my life, I was able to broach the subject about what had taken place between us years back. Unfortunately, the conversation would be abruptly interrupted and we would never come back to finish it, yet there seemed a mutual understanding that there was more to both of our stories than either of us knew, and what had happened was the by-product of the pain and problems that were embedded in our lives at that time. I am convinced today that both of my cousins had been molested as well. They had spent more time with the uncle who had molested me than I had. I don't believe that sexual abuse just comes out of the air.

But again, just as with my first experience with abuse, who could I have told? Who was going to come to my rescue? Would it have made any difference if I had shared my pain? I believe that part of the reason I became so private and went inside of myself is because I had watched my mother suffer in silence. With all of the fights and bruises, no one had come to fight for her, so I lived believing that I, too, had to suffer in silence and bare my pain alone.

Dr. Nikita C. Garris-Watson

Stepped On - The Straw that Broke the Camel's Back

My mother and her husband, Stanley, met through his sister; they worked together at the IRS. We were living with my uncle in Petersburg, but we would drive back and forth to Richmond to go to school. After only knowing my mother for a very short time, he had wrote a long letter to me telling me how much he loved me and would buy me things. How he would never hurt my mother like the others. How he would protect her. My response to the letter must not have been too favorable because I remember being corrected for being "rude." I later learned as an adult looking back on this moment that I was being discerning, not disrespectful. I simply did not trust him or his spirit.

After years of living in a house filled with arguments fights, confusion and increased poverty, it happened the May following my 12th birthday. Again, it was the middle of the night and my little sister was sound asleep in the other twin bed. I was asleep too, and then I felt a hand in my underwear. I remember thinking that that couldn't be because neither my cousin nor my uncle was there. Then I thought maybe I was having a nightmare, which was not uncommon for me. Snatched from my sleep, I simply couldn't make sense of what was happening, but my first instinct was to check on my sister; thankfully, when I looked over at her, she was sound asleep.

Then I felt these hands on me again and a voice whispered harshly, "Be quiet. Don't say nothing. It's alright." But, of course, it wasn't alright. Laying on the floor next to my bed was my step-father, Stanley. He was lying on his side. He reached up and pulled down my panties while getting up on his knees in an effort to get

20

into my bed. I could smell the distinct stench of marijuana and alcohol coming from his body. Just then the hall light came on and he scrambled to lie down flat. It was my mother going to the bathroom. The light was shining through her gown. I could see the silhouette of her pregnant body as she went into the bathroom. She was carrying his child. When she closed the door to the bathroom, he quickly left my room. It was Friday.

On Saturday, I was recluse. I did not want to go anywhere near him. The next day, Sunday, my mother took me, my brother and two younger sisters to church, which was odd because we rarely, if ever, went to church. He stayed behind, though, so it was just us. We had been invited by the cousins of my sister's biological father. I don't remember what the pastor preached, but I was sitting in the back of the church. I remember this sense of urgency – a pull/draw – to go to the altar. When I got to it, I fell on my knees, and I wept and wept. I wept for so many reasons. I had not been saved yet; I had only been to church as a small child with my foster grandmother; since that time, I had attended once with my adopted aunt and twice with my sister's biological grandparents. I found that during each visit to church, although few and far between, I longed to know God to understand why others had a god and I did not.

I literally wanted to die. I didn't want to have to tell anybody what had happened to me or to deal with the mess that would come behind telling. I knew before I even opened my mouth that I was going to be called a liar. Even in the smallest things, my mother had always taken the side of whatever male had been in her life at that moment against me – us. And I hated Stanley, profusely. I hated him for what he represented. I hated him because he was yet another person who had abused my mother. I hated him because he had gotten her pregnant for a second time, and felt like when that happened, we all got trapped. He was also seven years younger than my mother, so I always believed that he was unqualified to be in our lives.

So when I went to the altar, I wanted to die because I didn't want to deal with what was coming next. I didn't want to deal with telling the story or facing my mother, the rejection. I did not want to deal with any of that. I didn't want to be hated by the one person who I wanted to love me more than anything. I was angry because every time she had a child or got into another relationship, I lost another piece of her. So I kept dealing with the shame and secrets. I had a mother, but I was a motherless child. I had been forced to grow up way ahead of time. Forced to deal with adult feelings and emotions. Forced to hold secrets. There was no safe place, not even in my own mind. Somebody had to be doing something. Hopelessness had surrounded me from the beginning. While this incident only happened once, and didn't involve penetration and certainly paled in comparison to the repeated violations that I had been enduring since the age of six, it was by no means acceptable. Furthermore, after having been molested from six until 12, I had decided that I couldn't stand having another person take anything from me anymore.

After we left church, when we got home, I asked my mother if I could tell her something. We were living in a 3-level townhouse then. The bottom level was the basement; my step-father smoked marijuana down there frequently. In fact, he always wreaked of it: even that night I told my mother what he had done.

We sat down in the living room area and I told her what had happened. She said, "Go to your room. Let me talk to him and I'll come and get you." Even though I was in my room on the floor, and they were down in the basement, I could hear the screaming and hollering.

He screamed vehemently, "That little bitch is lying!"

She came back up to the room, but there was no meeting, so I never got the chance to confront him. She told me that she needed to think about some things. That was Sunday evening. I went to school on Monday (the next day) and I told a counselor because I knew nothing was going to be done about it. She wasn't going to protect me. So I told. I would never have the chance to go back home after that night. I never had the chance to hug my brother and sisters goodbye. I didn't get to pack my things, and when I did finally get them, they were stuffed into black trash bags. I felt like the trash that gets left at the curb. The next time I would see my mother's face would be in the courtroom. The only sound I would have of her voice would be that of angry accusations, a voice riddled with hate. We would end up in court behind the charges and I would again know how it felt to feel betrayed and abandoned by my mother.

After the big blow up, initially, I was sent to live with Aunt Mary. As a part of the process, I was subjected to several attorneys' interviews and even a lie detector test. Everyone believed me except for my own mother, but the true irony of the situation was that the very aunt who was protecting me from my mother's husband, didn't know that her own son had also been molesting me for years or that her younger brother was the first one to have violated me. She would later learn some of these details, but not all. I did not have the heart to tell her everything. So it was trying to keep these secrets from her that ignited my request to live with someone else. I simply didn't want to live under their roof and risk nightly rapes over and over again.

The first time I faced my mother in court was in Virginia Beach where she basically gave me over to Aunt Sally who was also my godmother as I mentioned earlier. There was no fight on her part; she was pregnant with my youngest brother and she just didn't even fight for me. She gave my godmother custody of me and left without saying one word to me. In retrospect, if you can't protect yourself, you can't protect others. My mother was being abused and had lived a life of continuous abuse. There was really no way she could have protected me even if she had wanted to.

Dr. Nikita C. Garris-Watson

Consistently Inconsistent

"Sometimes God doesn't change your situation because He's trying to change your heart" (Unknown).

Going to church had been a hit and miss experience for me. After leaving my grandmother's house at the age of three, only on rare occasions would I see the inside of a church. Surprisingly, it was at church where I got the courage to tell my mother what had happened to me at the hands of her brother and her husband as mentioned in the previous chapter. One particular Sunday, I went to church with my grandmother, and I can recall sitting on the wooden pews in church with a sense that I needed something. I had not yet realized that the "something" was really a "someone" who would change my very existence. I listened to the preacher that morning with a greater feeling of urgency as I peeked at those in the pews around me. I could hear the preacher, but my heart seemed to hear words that were not to be spoken aloud. I would catch snatches of the message, but of all that was said that day, I would only remember a promise of help. I knew that with all that I was facing, I needed help and I needed it fast.

When the offer for salvation was given, I paused for a moment in doubt that it was truly available to me. I distinctly remember sitting on the edge of the pew and then sliding back thinking, no not me. Before I could make sense of what was happening, I was at the front of the church on my knees weeping for God to save me. I only had a rudimentary understanding of what "saved" meant, but if it was the opportunity for help, I knew I needed. If being saved would rescue me from the daily torment that I was feeling, I wanted this help. Perhaps I would get help to sleep at night. Help to not feel like my heart was breaking each day. Help to not hate myself. Help to understand why my mother did not believe me. Help to take the pain away.

My grandmother would join me at the altar to pray for me and to be a part of my salvation confession. I would find myself whisked away to a back room, my clothes changed into all white and then being led to the Baptism pool. Right before being immersed in the water, I recall wondering if I would finally feel clean from the repeated violations, from the memories of the verbal and physical abuse, from the abandonment and rejection that had pierced my soul. Walking home from church that day, I knew that my life would never be the same, yet, my salvation experience would lead me to more questions than answers that would take years to reconcile.

My life did not magically change after that simply because I had been saved; my problems, issues and behaviors were soon becoming *too* much for my Aunt Sally to the point where it was interfering with the raising of her only daughter who was younger than me. I was mouthing off and would go outside and talk to the boys on the corner. I would also have boys come over after school and hang out in front of the house when she was still at work. My moods were not consistent even though I was quiet and would withdraw to my room a lot. It was all just too much for her to handle.

However, my aunt didn't give me back to my mother because the case against my step-father had not come up yet, and legally, I was not able to go back to my mother's home. I believe she felt that I needed a more supervised environment. So during the Christmas break of 1987, I went to live with my grandmother for the second time in my life. It would be my fifth home and the third school in less than a year.

Dr. Nikita C. Garris-Watson

The oldest of eleven siblings and the mother of six adult children, my grandmother had a huge family that visited a lot. It was strange to me at first because I did not understand the family dynamics. She would cook and people would come over or visit, so I stayed in my room a lot because I was uncomfortable. I attempted to avoid these family interactions because internally, I felt like a reject and an outcast, and that people knew my story and so looked at me with repulsion or suspicion. While they actually treated me warmly, I could not reconcile what I saw with what I was feeling. I was in torment.

In going to live with Grandma Greene, I was introduced to things that I had never seen. I saw a different dynamic of family. The Greene's were a really large family and were very loving to one another – they still are. Prior to my grandfather's death, he and my grandmother had been married for over 50 years. I never saw them argue during the time that I lived with them. So to go from a house where almost daily I witnessed physical fights to a place where I didn't see any arguments at all was shocking. My mother, her sister-in-laws and Aunt Mary would always go through this cycle of fights and brokenness. One day, they were thick as thieves, and the next, they were cussing each other out. And so to get to my grandmother's house and see siblings who talked to one another all of the time and who genuinely loved each other, it was so confusing and different for me.

The adjustment period was awkward and difficult to articulate when I first moved in with my grandmother. I would stay in my room because the behavior in the Greene home was so uncomfortable for me. I did not know how to respond to that environment. My grandmother has always been very loving and engaging, so she would always take people in and take care of folks that didn't even belong to her or her family.

Groups of people would literally come over to the house every Sunday to eat. I had never seen anything like this! I saw that people could actually love each other in a healthy way, but I could not seem to find a way to become *that* or even be a part of it. Again, it was like I wanted something that was outside of my grasp. I was just so broken and damaged. I could see them, but the wall around me kept me at a distance mentally and emotionally.

So there I was in a new school, trying to adjust, and although I was living in a familiar house with my grandmother (I had lived there with her from birth to three years old), everything was strange to me; it was a very difficult time. My grandmother hadn't had me in her home since I was three, and so she did not know who I was now at 13. She had only seen me a few times since I was a toddler. That is a huge gap in years in terms of development mentally and physiologically. I was no longer a cute little-girl child who wanted to color or play with dolls. I was now a child who had been violated in ways no human should ever be. I was messed up, but my grandmother did the best that she could with me.

I remember one day when we had just finished picking collard greens and were snapping green beans at the kitchen table, she finally asked me what had happened to me. First of all, it was really strange for me to tell her. I hesitated to give any details because I was so used to having to hide the secrets of my past and live under the shadow of the shame of my memories. I was sure that if she knew my hidden truths, that she would view me differently, perhaps even question her love for me. I sat there pondering what to share and what to keep to myself. But as I snapped the beans, I told her what I could, and it was like I was being transported back to several moments of my life all at once.

I was snapping peas, pulling out memories and crying simultaneously. With snap of a pea, I was snapping open the dark secrets of my life. I could feel the energies of my abusers all around me. It was like I was there again…with each one. With each pop of the pea, pain pierced my memory. When I finished telling what I could handle telling her in that moment, I looked at my grandmother and I could see that her eyes were wet. She said, "Baby, that's a lot for one person."

A few short months later, we went to court. The night before, I had picked out all black to wear because that was how I felt: dead. Grandma said, "You can't wear that." I tried to argue with her at first because I really wanted to wear all black and I could not understand why she would not let me. Looking back on it, I realize that I was in mourning. She won, of course, and made me wear a white dress instead. I found it ironic to be made to wear white when I felt so dirty. I would dress that morning slowly, not ready to publicly tell the world what had happened to me. I wasn't ready to tell the secrets.

When I walked into the courtroom after having been sequestered for a while, I saw that my Aunt Sally and Aunt Mary were there. Grandma Greene did not come with me; a great woman of peace, it would have torn her heart to witness those she loved, for I knew she loved my mother, too, at war with one another. Also present was my mother, Stanley and other family members. They all sat behind my mother; no one sat on my side of the court behind me. I felt like everyone was against me, which in many ways was true.

When it was my turn to be questioned, I told the court my story. I told the judge, though, that when I was being touched, I thought that I was dreaming because I had been asleep prior to my mother's husband coming into the room. I continued to explain the rest of what had taken place that night up to the point where my mother had turned on the hall light. Then his lawyer was given permission to ask me questions that I answered without hesitation and as truthfully as I could. The series of questions made it appear as if I was actually the one on trial and not the other way around. The results would follow that same pattern; after I was removed from the courtroom, the judge found my abuser not guilty.

The irony of the situation is that Stanley had refused to take a lie detector test prior to the court date, but I took it and passed. The officer and court appointed attorney both told me that they believed my story. I had told the truth as proven by the lie detector test and even in the courtroom, but it was not good enough for my family or the court. I can honestly say that after hearing about the verdict, I gave up that day. Nothing mattered anymore, not even my grades. They would drop right along with my spirit.

I was subsequently returned to my grandmother, and things became even worse for me. I didn't want to listen to anyone or obey any rules. For instance, the summer prior to my senior year, I had taken a job with Burger King at Fort Lee, and I wanted to work as many hours as I could. My grandmother told me no because it was not acceptable for a young girl to work extremely late or be out past certain a time, especially on a military base. I raised my voice back at her in defiance. I wanted to do what *I* wanted to do. What did it matter, I thought? No one cared for me anyway, right? No one cared anything about me.

A few days later, I learned that my grandmother had been taken to the hospital complaining of chest pains. I immediately wanted to go see her, but was told no because I was not allowed to visit. With the hospital being within walking distance, I contemplated being defiant and going anyway until I received a phone call from my grandmother's daughter. She said to me, "If anything happens to my mother, I'll kill you." Life was over for me again as I knew it. I was soon sent back to my mother's home, which was the last place I wanted to be and needed to be at that point in my life. It was there that I would try to kill myself … for the second time.

Dr. Nikita C. Garris-Watson

Chapter 3 ~ Hell on Earth

"Hopelessness is forgetting help is on the way"
(Unknown).

Dying isn't that Easy

The first time I tried to take my life, I was 10 years old. After a fight with my mother and my step-father, I tried to run away, but was snatched back into the house and locked in my room. Family members were due to come over for some family function, and even though it had been a traumatic fight, they did not cancel it. When I was allowed to go to the bathroom, I grabbed the first bottle of pills that I could find and tried to swallow all of them. My cousin came in just as I was swallowing the pills and quickly went and told her mother what I was doing. I remember my mother came into my room fussing and hollering at me. Just as in the near drowning incident years before, her response was not that of a mother who cared, in my opinion; instead, her verbal response was that I had been "looking at too much TV" and was just doing "stupid stuff" to get attention. She didn't even take me to the hospital to make sure that I was okay.

After being sent to back my mother's house following the hospitalization of my grandmother, which was the summer prior to my senior year, I would end up fighting with my mother and Stanley once again. I hated everything about being back in their house and they used every opportunity to let me know that it was my fault that I was there, and that nobody wanted me. I overheard conversations where he would state, "That lying bitch does not need to be here."

I slept on a couch, my clothes and other personal things in trash bags next to me. I was not able to talk to any of those I called friends from where my grandmother lived because it was long distance; I was stuck. I plotted to run away, but I had no idea where I would go.

Feeling hopeless after the fight, I grabbed my bible and ran into the bathroom. I sat on the floor next to the toilet weeping in agony. I decided that death was the only way out of my living hell. I searched the medicine cabinet for pills, but I couldn't find any, so I grabbed a razor from under the sink and began to scrape my wrists with the blades hoping to cut myself deep enough to bring death. Blood splattered onto the *Bible* in my lap as tears filled my eyes. I wanted out of this life so badly. I cried out, "God, if you are real, let me die! Right here! Right now!" My mother, probably hoping to finish the fight which had precipitated all of this, forced her way into the bathroom and found me on the floor bleeding. Instead of taking me to the emergency room, I was taken to a mental health hospital in the middle of the night.

My first thought upon arrival was, 'Yeah! I have officially gone crazy." And, again, my mother's actions confirmed that perhaps I was. She ended up leaving me in the mental health hospital by myself. I was 16 years old.

There were two sides to the hospital. On one side was long-term care and mental health patients, and the other was short-term care and drug users who were in the midst of withdrawal. PCP and LSD was hitting the community really hard at that time, and I remember that there were so many kids who were there going through drug withdrawals. When some of them would go into withdrawal fits or hallucinations, strangely, many of them would come to me when I called out their names; they'd sit down beside me and then calm down and begin to pour out their hearts - telling me their stories - without hesitation. Keep in mind that everything we did was observed by the staff or recorded by the many cameras that surrounded us. I don't know how or why, but they began to record how these kids were responding to me. During my one-on-one sessions with the counselors, they would let me read some of the notes written about me. The common thread from those who had observed me was that while I could not or would not freely share my thoughts with the staff or deal with what was happening to me, it appeared that I could help other people.

The truth is that I did not know how to deal with my problems. I had been keeping secrets all of my life. They were telling me to talk, but I had learned that if I talked, I would be punished or sent away. It was the summer between my junior and senior year in high school, and I agonized over what would happen to me if I did share what I was feeling or what had happened to me. What more could they do to silence me if I told? They made us write down our feelings and thoughts, and that was not safe for me, so I never wrote down too much. I kept my comments brief and superficial, but they needed more from me. I had no emotions in my writings, they'd say. But emotions had never helped me; crying had never helped me. So why show them anything, was my attitude.

What I know now is that I had a false sense of strength in believing that *not* telling my story - neither writing it down nor showing emotion - would keep me safe from harm. I simply had to disconnect in order to survive and not lose my mind most of my life. It had become the only thing I knew to do to save myself. Yet, I had this uncanny ability to be open enough - present-minded - that these deeply troubled kids would gravitate to me. So as a part of my treatment, they began to allow me to sit with other kids and talk to them, but only if I also talked about my feelings with the therapist. In other words, I could help somebody as long as I talked. Little did I know that this was not only going to lead me down the road to the journey of healing, but also to my destiny.

While I was in the institution, my mother never came to see me. I was there for two months with no visitors. Residents were supposed to have consistent family visits as part of practice and hospital policy as it related to patient care, but no one came to see me. I remember that they tried to call my mother once, but her phone was disconnected. I felt a deeper sense of abandonment; if I never felt it before, I most assuredly felt it then.

She finally did call, though; in fact, she called two times. The first time she called, after I hung up, I literally flipped my mattress over in a fit of rage and punched the mess out of it. The conversation with her consisted of her screaming, "Why do you have these people calling me at my job about you!?" When she would finally call again a few weeks later, I was in the lunch line and they told me that I had a phone call. I picked it up and she literally started cussing me out.

"You got these people looking for me! I got four kids that I need to take care of…" She actually had five children, if you included me; I guess in her mind, I was already dead. I didn't matter enough for her to even come and see me. "You are not gonna waste my time with this foolishness!" she screamed over the line and slammed the phone down. She never came to see me during my extended hospital stay. In fact, it would be three years after that call when I would speak to my mother again.

Things got so bad for me after call that due to the stress of my situation, my hair started to fall out in chunks. Thankfully, one of the clinicians got permission to take me home to get my hair done and I was able to get my hair braided. When my psychiatrist learned the full gravity of the situation - the lack of any visitors, the inability to locate my mother after the last phone call, the hair loss and the need for a plan for my release (either to family or foster care) - he pressed the hospital to find my grandmother who had come up in several of our sessions together. They found her and my aunt after I was finally able to give them their phone numbers, and told them about what was happening to me. They were shocked.

I would learn later on that my mother had sent a letter to my grandmother telling her that I was doing well and progressing, but she had neglected to mention that she had not visited me since I had been institutionalized. Ironically, just days before the letter arrived, the institution had already contacted my grandmother and informed her that I had technically been abandoned. My mother had been caught in a lie. I never knew how it was addressed or handled by my grandmother, but they now knew the truth. The institution convinced my grandmother to take me back with the understanding that I would still be getting treatment.

Here is how God works. I was not insured the entire time that I was in the mental health facility. Unbeknownst to me, my psychiatrist had agreed to continue to see me without insurance – for free – because I needed treatment. I **NEEDED** treatment. I saw him once a month until I graduated from high school six months later, and although that was not a lot of time for extensive treatment, it was enough to get me through moments where I needed to progress.

Sadly, I do not remember my psychiatrist's name, but this doctor was a wonderful person. I remember once during a session before my discharge, he ordered pizza for us to share during session probably just so that I could have something positive going on for the moment. He even sent me a graduation card. I will forever cherish what he did for me, but even more importantly, how he treated me like a human being. You don't meet people like this too often who just genuinely care about you.

Still, my demons were not fully gone yet. I would try to take my own life again when I was 17 years old and about to leave for college. Following high school graduation, I found myself back at my mother's house with no future in sight, working a dead end job at a restaurant. I am sure my grandmother thought that time with my mother would heal the broken relationship, but it only made things worse with each return to her house. I was, again, in a place of hopelessness. I thought that I was never going to get away from my mother; I didn't want to be like her. At one point, I even thought that I wasn't going to be able to go to the college that I was now preparing to leave for. I was upset also that my time was up with my grandmother and I was not yet able to live on my own. Although I had a job, I didn't make enough to where I could take care of myself. I didn't have a place to go, but I knew where I didn't want to be; my mother's house was never the place I wanted to find myself at again. My thoughts were in such chaos. Depression was still a daily demon that chased me relentlessly. I truly believed that there was really no reason to live and that no one would miss me if I were gone.

Since cutting my wrists did not work the first time, I decided to take a couple of bottle of pills I had found in the medicine cabinet. I ended up swallowing the contents of two bottles. I balled myself up in the corner waiting on death to finally greet me. My mother would find me like this, and unlike when I was 10, she *had* to take me to the hospital. But I didn't die. Instead, I slept and then I woke up, nauseous, but still alive. "How can this be? Why am I still here? What will it take for me to die?" I said to myself. I could not even die right. Sadly, I would try to take my life one more time, but this time, the end result would not be a hospital stay. Instead, it would bring me to my destiny.

Chapter 4 ~ Daddy Damage

"When my mother and father forsake me, then the Lord will take me up" (Psalm 27:10).

Nobody's Little Girl

The absence of a father – not knowing who my real father is even at my current age – has played a big part in the decisions I've made in my life. Not having a father present in your life is painful enough, but then, when you have these substitute fathers who do nothing but cause more pain, it becomes a kind of double injury: double damage. We choose the people in our lives based on our experiences or we choose people based on what we hope they can be. The latter leads to unrealistic expectations. That was the problem I had with my first husband. I wanted him to be perfect. I wanted him to make me feel better. I wanted him to make me feel beautiful. I wanted him to fulfill a role in my life that he was not qualified to handle.

In other words, I wanted my first husband to do the things that my father should have done and ultimately what only God can do. So I entered into the relationship with a lot of unrealistic expectations on my part for him, which in hindsight was unfair to him both as a person and a man. While most people say that they don't care that they didn't have a father growing up, or that you really grow to not care, most of your life, there's always something that reminds you that you are *the* child without a father or that you're the child that does not have *someone* to call "daddy."

What truly made the situation worse for me, I believe, is that up until the age of seven, I was convinced that my sister's father, Matthew, was my biological dad, too. However, one day, my mother allowed Jerome to talk her into telling me that he was not. Jerome was the relationship in between my sister's father and my mother's current husband, Stanley. He was the one who beat me for nearly drowning. Before him, there were only a few sporadic dates here and there, but for the most part, my mother spent many years in unhealthy, abusive situations, and this man was one of those. He was a cruel, abusive man, as I mentioned earlier in my story and will more soon.

I would not wish for the way in which I learned that I did not have a father on my worst enemy. We were living in Church Hill on 24th Avenue with my Aunt Mary at the time, and my mother called me downstairs to the living room. When I entered into the room, she proceeded to say, "I have something I need to tell you."

She was speaking slowly and softly about "my father" when Jerome forcefully took over the conversation and abruptly exclaimed, "He is not your father!"

I remember initially not understanding how that could be or what the news meant for me. I do know that when I asked why I had been lied to and who my real father was, I was met with evasive answers and a 'we will talk about it later.' That talk never happened and I would be left searching for understanding even today.

None of my memories of her interactions with Matthew are violent; he was the first person that I called "Dad" and actually still do whenever we interact, which is not as often as I'd like for it to be. I was still allowed to go with my sister to Matthew's family's house afterwards and would see him as occasions permitted; however, after that incident, I never felt that I belonged to any family. No one could or would quite answer my questions about my parentage.

Dr. Nikita C. Garris-Watson

While the issue of my biological father certainly remains a mystery still, my sister's father has been there for me at key points in my life. Therefore, I view him as a father, but often with a sense of subtle disconnect because of not feeling like his *real* daughter. Once when I discussed this situation with his older sister, she shared with me that when I was conceived, he sincerely thought that I was his, but that he had been convinced after I was born that I was not. I never understood why he didn't settle the matter for sure with a paternity test, but I suspect that this was because he had not withdrawn from the relationship immediately after I was born. I have since deduced, however, that because he was from an affluent black family and headed for a stellar military career, my mother and I didn't fit into that picture, so he left things alone. A future military officer being tied to a poor woman from a broken family and a child out of wedlock would not have helped to advance his career. This situation would be further compounded by the birth of my sister who is without a doubt his biological daughter.

Although Matthew would try to fill that role of "father," because of the animosity between him and my mother, coupled with his frequent military travel, she began to use my sister and I as pawns between the two of them. My mother would get angry with him and not allow us to see him. When they were on good terms, then we could see him. Again, we became pawns in this sick game of 'if you don't love me, or do what I want, then you can't see the kids.' As such, I never really got the chance to consistently develop a relationship with him, which created a disconnection between us, but the sad part is that neither did my sister, his biological daughter. For my sister, the back and forth between our mother and her father created a difficulty for her because she could not understand why her own father was not fully present in her life, and it wasn't that he didn't truly want to be present. He didn't want to have to keep fighting our mother.

Consequently, because of the immaturity of both of her parents, she would struggle to get to know him, but this is her story to tell for her book. The bottom line is that in watching how these two "grown" people interacted with one another, what I began to learn was that when people love each other, the think they are the best person in the world, but when they break up, they try to make each other look like the worst people in the world.

With regard to the identity of my own father, there is a great debate regarding this. It seems to be my mother's big secret. She would tell me that he is my now deceased Aunt Priscilla's brother, Jeff. Again, I called "aunt" more so because she was my mother's best friend, not because of any family relations. New information regarding this situation would come to me the summer after my first year of college. I received a call from her one day. She said she wanted to talk to me about some things. (I'd later learn that she had cancer, so perhaps she was just trying to clear her heart or some things in her life before she passed away.)

Aunt Priscilla and I proceeded to discuss what my life was like; we talked about my goals and dreams and then the subject of her brother came up. She shared that she loved me and would always treat me like her niece. She explained that she was torn about believing that I was her brother's child because if I was, she believed that he would have had stepped up to the plate and claimed me as well as taken care of me. She talked about not understanding why I had not been treated fairly regarding many situations and often wondered if I would make it through life. My aunt then went on to say that she always knew that I was smart and that I would either fulfill my dream of becoming a judge or end up in front of one. I laughed as I listened to her share her memories with me. Finally, she said that even though she was not sure if I were her niece, she would treat me like I was anyway so that if it came out one day that I was, then she would have done right by me, and if I weren't, she still had done right by me.

I had been sitting at the dining room table and I remember sitting in the dark for a long time after that conversation trying to make sense of the conversation – of my life. Internally, it felt like my heart and chest were on fire. Tears would not be my comfort that day; only emptiness and deeper pain. It was good to know that she loved me as if I were her blood family, but it hurt more so to know that I was truly *not* connected to anyone biologically. Another wall of defense went up that day.

A year later, when I was 19 or so, I learned that Aunt Priscilla's mother was in the hospital battling a terminal illness. I had only spent a little time with her throughout the years, but each encounter was positive. While talking with my cousin, the daughter of my aunt and a frequent childhood companion, I decided to show my support just for a moment knowing that this process would be hard for all of them. I learned that Jeff (the man everyone suspected was my father) was at the hospital as well. Before I went to the hospital, I suggested that this would be a good time to get closure for everyone so that their mother could have some peace; since she was in the hospital, my theory was that we could do a DNA test then and there, and be done with the years of confusion; they all agreed.

By the time I arrived at the hospital, Jeff had departed. It was explained to me that he was afraid to meet me and didn't want to deal with the situation. My response was that I was too old for back child support and getting closure would take away his fears. His mother expressed her disappointment at what had taken place and she tried to make me feel better. I explained to her that she was not at fault and no one could be forced to face anyone or anything that they were not ready to. Truthfully, all I had wanted of him was to settle once and for all who was or was not my father. But it was not to be that day, or even to this day.

At the age of 25, I fell ill; I was diagnosed with hyperthyroidism. After many doctors' visits and other health complications, one of the concerns of my husband at the time was that I couldn't provide my doctor with a complete family medical history. Therefore, he insisted that I reach out to my "natural" father to get details about any hereditary conditions in the family. I wrote the letter and sent it to the address of my said biological father with hopes that it would reach him for clarity and explanation. I explained in the letter that I was not asking him for anything but a DNA test to clear up the confusion, and if the results came back positive that he was my father, then I would need a list of medical conditions that ran in his family. I was very specific in explaining that I was dealing with some health issues and just needed to get a better idea as to whether it was all generational.

Six months went by with no response, so I reached out to his father to see if he had received the letter. I was told that Jeff did not want to meet, but that based on what he knew, the medical issue of hyperthyroidism did not exist in his family. Clearly, my supposed father had read or was given the letter to read. I was disappointed not that he didn't respond personally, but more so, that I would have to live with the unknown for the rest of my life. At the same time, I was angry with my then husband for forcing me to waste my time on a situation that I had always felt was hopeless. It would further damage my respect for his advice in the future.

Up until this day, my mother has talked very little about the situation regarding the paternity of my father to me. I've come to learn that there was apparently more than one person that she was dealing with at the time I was conceived. In short, I do not know whose sperm hit the egg first. It's a terrible joke that I often tell, but it is essentially true because I do not know who my father is. I believe that one of the reasons my mother is afraid to tell me what happened is that she is embarrassed. She has not alluded to whether or not she was forced to have sex or if it was her choice, but whatever the memories are surrounding my conception, it is so much so that she cannot talk to me about it.

And therein lies one of the many issues between me and my mother. There was no way I could ask my mother as I was growing about relationships and men because I would look at what she was doing with her own life and run the other way. She went from one abusive relationship to the next, never truly confronting the nexus of it all. Hence, as I began to grow and develop into a young woman, there was really no one to show me how to do this or say that when it came to establishing a strong, healthy relationship with a partner, and on an even deeper level, with myself. I look back on our life and I wonder if my mother has ever really had the chance to be happy?

Dr. Nikita C. Garris-Watson

Fighting Me Internally

One of my most painful memories is that of my mother being raped. During one of her many break-ups with Jerome, for a reason I do not quite remember, he called her and asked her to pick him up from somewhere. Despite being apart, she agreed to go and get him. When we pulled up to the location, he got in and then proceeded to take my little brother out of the backseat and put him on his lap, which was out of character for him. Then suddenly, a man with a gun jumped into the backseat of the car with me and my sister.

The gunman made my mom drive to an old, abandoned house. When we got there, he made me, my sister and my brother sit in one room and he took our mother and her "ex-boyfriend" to another room. What happened next was unthinkable. I literally heard Jerome rape my mother at gunpoint. She was raped repeatedly. I could hear her whimpering and crying in the other room, but not screaming. I remember wanting to scream, but I could not cry as much as I wanted to because my siblings were there with me. I didn't want to upset them and I was afraid that if we cried too much, he would have us killed.

During the entire rape, the gunman stood at the doorway with the gun pointed between us and them. At some point, my siblings had to go to the bathroom. I actually had to ask someone with a gun in my face for permission to take my baby brother and sister to the bathroom. I took them and I remember thinking, "What am I going to do?" I couldn't cry because I had to protect them, so I kept quiet. The bathroom was old with paint chipping and wallpaper peeling off of the walls. The toilet had a rust ring around it and everything was dirty. The window had no curtain and it was broken at the left corner. The only clean thing in the bathroom was the toilet paper. Even the soap in the sink was grimy. There were no towels or even a shower curtain. Nothing about the place felt right.

I wanted to take my siblings and run, but what would happen to my mother, I thought?
After they finished with her, would they kill her? If I took my siblings back into the room, would I be next? Did they plan to kill all of us? I didn't want to take my sister and brother back in that room, but I couldn't leave my mother alone even if I couldn't save her.

When he finally let us go, my mother immediately called the police. My head was throbbing with pain, my stomach was cramping and I had a fever; all I wanted to do was ball up in a knot and cry, but the police were asking me questions about the gunmen because I was the oldest: "Do you remember his face?" they asked. I tried to recall details, but I could only tell them very little: a short, thin, brown-skinned man with a little hair and dark eyes.

Jerome claimed that the gunman forced him to rape my mother. I knew that this man, who had beaten my mother senseless on so many occasions, could not be forced to do anything he did not want to. It was also odd to me that on that day when he got into the car prior to the gunman, he had reached back to pick up my brother and hold him in his lap. I found it also strange that my mother could only whimper; she never screamed during her assault, but then I realized that if she had screamed, she could have potentially cost us our lives.

As I replayed that horrific day over and over again in my head as I got older, I became convinced that it was all Jerome's doing. If you are afraid, how can someone force you into having an erection? He had set our mother up. I thought about how little he cared not just for my mother, but for his own biological son that was in the car and made to be a part of the situation.

Dr. Nikita C. Garris-Watson

Despite the awful incident, my mother would enter back into this on again, off again tortuous relationship. What should have been the end after her rape only became a cycle of beatings and brokenness that would replay itself over and over for years to come. He would haunt us at every turn and every place we would live. He would do more damage, physically and psychologically, to our family than ever should be experienced in a lifetime. I would see my mother bleeding and bruised, and wonder if we would ever escape the terror. She would escape from that abusive relationship eventually only to find herself trapped in another one, and this time, she'd never get away from that one.

I was no more than 9 or 10 when this rape occurred. One of the things I learned from this incident was how to be strong for other people and to suppress my own feelings and emotions early in life (it would cost me dearly). I also learned years later that this event coupled with having been raped and molested at such a young age myself, perverted my view of sex; instead of it being about the beauty of intimacy, it became a temporary cure for loneliness or of creating a pseudo sense of closeness with another human being.

Sex became the only momentary semblance of closeness to a man that I would allow, and then when it was over, it was over because I had created few other expectations for the relationship and had no trust for anyone. Because I had watched my mother get into these physically abusive relationships where she would fight, be beaten, but then turn around and sleep with her abuser, I began to wonder if I should equate sex with love. The answer was no. That was not going to work for me. In my mind, I had decided I would not be anyone's victim, but what my mind said and what my reality was did not line up. I was trying to be hard, yet at every turn, I was looking for love and trying to cure the feeling of rejection that had buried itself deep inside my soul.

In essence, as I would begin having sexual relationships with men without the perceived burden of commitment, what I was really trying to do was take control of something that had always been controlled for me from the age of six to 13. So I was promiscuous not because I was a whore, but because I was trying to take control over my life – my body. Sex now became my decision - who I wanted to have it with and when - or so I thought. What I didn't understand then, though, was that I was trying to also find an intimacy and genuine closeness with a man that I had never experienced. It was difficult to realize that I only had a false sense of control when it came to sex because, in actuality, my pain was controlling me. I was doing myself more damage and this time, I was the one holding the "smoking gun" in my hand.

Dr. Nikita C. Garris-Watson

The 6-month Rule

What I now know is that trauma led me to develop a 6-month rule for relationships where if I was in a relationship and I felt like it was not going anywhere, meaning it/he was not making me feel wonderful, beautiful – great, even – I'd end it. I had this thing about enjoying the beginning of a relationship, the euphoria of the beginning of it when you don't know much about each other and you could enjoy one another. But once the romance was gone, then I was, too. It was the transitional period of romance to reality where you are now getting into knowing who we really are and perhaps examining emotions that most frightened me. I thought I knew what love was, but I didn't. I wanted to remember it the way I wanted to remember it. In truth, I didn't want to get close to anyone – be mentally and emotionally intimate – because I didn't feel clean. I felt dirty and scarred. That if they found out about my past – my truth as I saw it then – they would not want me anymore.

The few times I tried to be vulnerable, I realized that I had so many walls up that I could not really see out and it hurt to let anyone in. Because I was making choices with the intent of controlling everything connected to me, the results became more about me than being equally accommodating. I could only see through the filter of my pain, never with the idea of possibility. I entered every relationship looking for the end and what we look for we typically find. I would spend more time waiting for the end of the relationship than I did enjoying what the relationship had to offer. I was repeatedly setting myself up for failure.

Although my first marriage lasted nearly 14 years, it was within the first six months that the trouble I was looking for found its way to the forefront. The problem this time was that I continued on with the relationship and let six months turn into 14 years of fighting my brokenness and him trying to build what I/we thought was the ideal family. It clearly did not work. In the years between my divorce and remarriage, I was forced to face many things about myself and endure painful moments of self-realization for the sake of healing. I would come face-to-face with my own low self-esteem while fighting toe-to-toe with my messed up perspectives about sex and relationships. New and old pain would flood my mind simultaneously, but I had to face my reality if I wanted a better future.

Despite my tremendous growth in the area, it was in the first year of my current marriage where I would have to confront this area that still demanded my attention. Despite knowing that God had sent my husband to me, I was still holding onto damaged beliefs about the instability and longevity of relationships. My current husband, James, and I did not have sex with each other prior to getting married; this was very important to us both, but to me especially because I wanted to maintain the holiness that I had fought so hard to find. It was one of the best decisions I ever made.

James and I have been married now for over five years. After we celebrated the first year of our anniversary, it became our practice to take moments to assess where we were and where we wanted to be in our marriage. But it did not come easy for me. During our first assessment on that one year anniversary, I found it difficult to share with him where I wanted to be or what I expected in the coming years for our marriage. I could talk easily about where I saw him going or even what I was believing for his life, but when discussing my expectations, I was hesitant in my responses. My husband tenderly, but directly responded, "You're cheating me and us because you are living with the end of this marriage in mind." I wanted to argue and defend my position, but swiftly recognized that while it was my husband's lips moving, it was really the Holy Spirit speaking. Deliverance would not come easy, but it would come that night as I walked and cried out to God to deal with the root of my issue.

When James and I first met, during one of our many talks, he asked me the question: "Is there anything I'd do to you that would remind you of your past?" No one had ever asked me that. I had told him in previous conversations bits and pieces of my past, but not its entirety. When we met, I had already been preaching about these things, and he had heard those sermons, so he knew *some* things, but not *everything*. I had told him enough to help him understand the complexities of my character, but that was it. And now, here I was having to confront fully what I would come to call the "Daddy Damage." I had been living with the effects of this damage all of my life and if I wanted to make *this* relationship work, I needed to be healed completely.

The "Daddy Damage" is an area that I have found myself having to minister to with greater frequency over the years. Initially, it made no sense to me why this would be one of my major areas of focus, especially since I didn't have a stable or consistent father-daughter relationship with anyone during my life. What I have since come to understand is *that* is where the problem begins and someone has to step in to help deal with the root before there can be any change in the results.

The lack of a father, coupled with the messed up images that I had been subjected to while growing up, resulted in an expectation that every relationship would involve pain; that sex was a 'fix all' and that fighting was an acceptable response. This often happens to girls whose fathers are unknown or who know their fathers, but they are not participating in their lives. The result is a void in a girl's life when there is no "active" father present. The girls are at risk, consequently, of becoming intimate with men hoping to get that same closeness they are missing from their fathers. They are hoping to get some kind of connection because of the feelings of rejection and intense need to be wanted. This need was the foundation for my promiscuity in my teens and early adult years. I was looking to be wanted. In my mind, if a man slept with me, then it was misinterpreted as a deeper want for me. But I needed to control everything pertaining to that dynamic, hence, the 6-month rule. I wanted love and intimacy, but I was not willing to risk being rejected…again.

Compounding this issue was the fact that I never had the privilege of having a "first." I would hear people talk often about their first encounters with sex and the stories are almost romantic and bring back feelings of pleasure for them. I was robbed of that innocence; my "first" experience with sex was tainted. I didn't have the privilege of having such a beautiful "first." For years, I would battle with the feelings of shame as I considered myself to be damaged goods. Even when I was married to my first husband, I would approach intimacy under the shadow of feeling dirty. Low and dark lights were a requirement because I never wanted to be fully seen.

As a believer, these feelings would be compounded with guilt knowing that God had a different standard. I would find my greatest spiritual battle to be in this area for years as I fought with containing what was prematurely opened in my life. I would cry out to God on more than one occasion to take away my battle with the flesh and just let me finally live my life. Promises would be made and promises would be broken as I fought for control over my flesh, and it would take time to finally gain discipline over this area. Initially, victory would not be celebrated by years, but by hours, and then by days, weeks, months and then year by year. I would learn to eventually control what had once controlled me.

Dr. Nikita C. Garris-Watson

It was not until my current marriage that I fully enjoyed the untainted pleasure of physical intimacy and the feeling that it *was* pure. Prior to my internal healing, the only wise decisions that I made was that no matter what, I would not have kids by multiple partners and that I would not allow my kids to be treated the way that I had been (promises to myself that I have kept throughout the years). Being uncertain of my biological make-up shaped and molded how I handled my children's interaction with their father and even what I looked for in a male partner following my divorce. Despite my less than pleasant divorce from my first husband, I always stressed the importance of his role in our children's life in an effort to avoid them having to deal with the same internal damages that I faced. So, I made choices and decisions that didn't make sense to others for the sake of making sure they had a consistent relationship with their father. (I will talk more about this later on.)

In looking back on my decisions and behavior, I realize now how important it is for people to have an identity, but especially girls. The father-daughter relationship shapes what we accept into our lives; it shapes the boundaries we create with men. It determines how far we let people go with us; it determines how we measure love and how we interact with other people. Everything I ever learned about human interaction was either by mistake or chance. There was no one to guide me, even though I had a mother present in my life, but my mother couldn't be my guide because she didn't know how to be one; she was too consumed by her own worries and troubles.

However, I learned something from watching her and that was what I didn't want in a man. I became hard, establishing resolute ideas about what I would never do based on what I saw her do for someone, which I would come to learn was another wrong in and of itself. The truth is that, in reality, some of the sacrifices my mother made were not wrong. They were just made for the wrong person, and this is why "Daddy Damage" is one of the cornerstones of my ministry today. After nearly being destroyed by this deeply embedded negativity that sex is a "cure-all," God revealed to me the need to use my pain to push out my purpose. My destiny was waiting for me.

Chapter 5 ~ From the Hood to Hooded

"Now if any of you lacks wisdom, he should ask God, who gives to all generously and without criticizing, and it will be given to him" (James 1:5 HCSB).

School Diversion and Distress

Growing up, school was a place of escape and enemies, but after the verdict of Not Guilty in favor of my step-father, it was more difficult than ever to focus. However, once at grandma's home, I felt safer because I wasn't in the negative environment I was when at my mother's; I wasn't subject to abuse or even seeing abuse. So I was able to eventually get back up and get it together, but it had been a long time for me. Things had not been the same since elementary school, and when I think back upon it, something must have happened to me then as well.

In fact, I remember one incident when I attended Bellevue Elementary School where the school psychiatrist brought me to her office. I don't know what precipitated having to go to her office, but something must have happened in order for me to have been there. I remember that she had toys in her office and she kept asking me questions as I played with them. This was around the time of my first violation at the hands of Uncle Leroy, so perhaps I said or did something in class that made her try to talk to me. I would be called into the office a few more times over the next year as she continued to study my behavior and responses. I can imagine the difficulty she must have faced in trying to get a child challenged to be quiet to speak up about things happening at home.

Starting with the 5th grade, I would find myself in a different school every year until the 10th grade. Middle school was the worst. I was forced to stay home a lot in order to take care of my younger siblings. It was so hard for me because I never wanted to miss school, but I had missed so many days in the 7th grade that they wanted to hold me back. They sent a note home with me one day saying that if I missed one more day, then that was it; I was going to repeat the 7th grade. And it was not because of my grades that they were considering this drastic action, but because of my attendance. I did manage to get through, but not without finding myself in the counselor's office while they tried to make sense of all of my absences. I was being asked to defend decisions that I myself did not understand or agree with.

School was a double-edged sword for me on most days. Although I enjoyed learning, I hated the interaction with people and being joked on or talked about. It was too often a battlefield where I was forced to fight physically to defend my poverty and even to defend my intellectual abilities. When your desired safe place is also your place of struggle, it's difficult. I remember one time in the 5th grade when I overheard my teacher say to another, "Cute girl, but those are the ugliest shoes I've ever seen." I would shrink down under the weight of embarrassment trying not to allow the tears filling my eyes to be seen. On another occasion, in particular, I went to the library to check out the book, *The Diary of Ann Frank*, and was asked by the librarian if I could handle that reading or would I prefer an easier book.

Those two moments stuck with me, haunting me for much of my life, but I would not realize the extent of the damage of those moments until my late twenties as I stood in my closet with countless unworn shoes before me, some of them even duplicates. Outwardly, it seemed like just shoe love until the Holy Spirit nudged me. This was not love; this was an obsession and the root went back over 15 years. I would sit on the floor of my closet that evening and weep for the little girl that often didn't have more than one pair of shoes; and it was all because of that one pair that had brought shame to me. I had unknowingly allowed the words of that teacher to play out in my life in the form of impulse buying, but instead of tucking my head between my legs this time, I decided to face the pain head on.

With shoeboxes surrounding me on every side, I began to deal with the desire to have more shoes than I really needed. I would give away 75 pairs of shoes that weekend and instead of missing any of them, I walked away with something more: PEACE that I had not realized that I needed. While my love for pretty shoes has not disappeared, my ability to discipline my purchases has replaced my impulses. And even though my shoe collection is still taking up plenty of closet space, it is not taking up space in my heart or soul anymore.

But where school would fail me, reading would be my true escape from reality. I could be angry, but I'd use it as my escape to another world. I loved it! And my mother knew this, so whenever I was put on punishment, the punishment was not being allowed to read. I never really wanted to go outside and I didn't really watch TV, but I read. She'd make me take all of my books out of my room and I'd have to sit there in an empty room. It was painful; reading was a major part of why I loved school.

While I don't remember my mother attending many school events or supporting my involvement in extracurricular activities, there was an expectation that I was to bring home good grades. Her mantra was that we could not bring home anything below a B because C's were for average children and she didn't have any average children. This pressure to produce was both positive and negative; it raised the awareness of doing better, but it became agony when problems at home were consuming my mind and my ability to focus at school.

Changing schools every year only added to the turmoil of needing stability, yet at the same time, changing schools every year gave me the opportunity to not have to deal with the same bullies or teasers from the previous year. Still, I found that the worse life became, the more I went into a shell. I learned the art of being hidden in plain sight and how not to draw attention to myself. This would, at times, be misperceived as my being an easy target. For example, one time in particular, two girls threatened to beat me up after school the next day. I was vulnerable because I often walked home alone. I told my mother about the pending beat down and instead of allowing me to stay home from school, she stated, "If you don't fight, I'll beat you."

The agony of that night and what was going to happen the next day were fresh in my mind as I walked to school that morning; as promised, they approached me, and a fight that I didn't realize I had deep within me rose up. Perhaps I was fighting for all the times that I couldn't defend myself; perhaps I was fighting because I was afraid of the pending whipping at the hands of my mother if I didn't fight – and win! But fight I did that day. When I looked up, my older cousins were standing near the gate watching the entire debacle. I would later learn that they had been sent by my mother to watch and to even help me if needed. Although I didn't get a beating, something inside of me snapped and I found myself ready to fight at every turn if I needed to after that day. No longer was I afraid to defend myself, at least not in school. This is the place where I am sure a spirit of defense settled in that I would have to live with for years to come.

Dr. Nikita C. Garris-Watson

What was meant to teach me self-defense would become the problem that God would have to help me with over and over again. I had lived my life on the defense, constantly waiting for something to happen. I had approached all situations on the defensive expecting the worst of people and waiting to defend myself at every turn. I was argumentative and aggressive in countless situations as I aspired to "protect" myself from everyone and everything. Trust was non-existent and everyone was a suspect. Despite my outwardly quiet demeanor, lurking below the surface was bitterness and anger misdirected at anyone who *dared* disrespect me.

This picture of who I had become would be presented to me over and over again in my moments with God, and despite the overwhelming evidence that God was right, I even debated with Him the necessity for maintaining my defensive stance. There was no way that I could see taking down my guard and allowing people to walk all over me, but with each turn in life, God would have to show me how my walls were a weakness to my spiritual witness. It would not be an easy deliverance process because I wanted to hold on to my right to fight instinctively versus spiritually.

Year after year, God reminds me that He is in control and will cover me if I allow Him to. I still have my moments, but my greater defense is to lean on Proverbs 18:10: "The name of the LORD is a strong tower: the righteous runneth into it, and is safe." Now, am I still a fighter? Yes! But I fight with my faith instead of with my fists.

Thankfully, I would graduate a year early from high school even with all of my worries and troubles, and while my grandparents and other adopted family were present at the ceremony, my mother was nowhere to be found. In fact, five degrees later, she has never attended any of my graduations. I am reminded of the words of Reinhold Niebuhr containing the serenity prayer: "God grant me the serenity to accept the things I cannot change; courage to change the things I can; and wisdom to know the difference." These words have never been more personal for me when I think about my mother not being present at the most important events of my life.

Dr. Nikita C. Garris-Watson

The Fight to Finish – Undergrad

*"Success is not final, failure is not fatal: it is the
courage to continue that counts"
(Winston Churchill).*

Making it to college was nothing short of the
hand of God at work; nothing in me or around me
promoted post-secondary education as my next step after
high school. Although my mother stated she didn't raise
any average children, she also didn't push anything
beyond work after school. Instead, I was being filled
with the idea that there was no hope for me. Even with
the love of my grandmother, she knew that she could not
afford to send me to college. I wanted to be a lawyer and
a judge to help children like me, but I dared not dream
that I could really ever become one.

During my junior year of high school, our school
librarian had arranged a trip to take students on a college
tour including to her Alma Mater in North Carolina. I
would walk across the campuses in awe of what I saw,
and not just the buildings, but seeing those who were
black like me getting an education. I would hear student
after student talk about where they were from and how
they got to school, yet I dared not even think that I would
be able to be one of them. I remember sitting in awe at a
Step Show on one of the campuses, and my heart longed
to enjoy the experience, but I quickly quieted my spirit
so that disappointment would not be my story again.

The dream of school would seem even further
from me the summer following my junior year when my
behavior resulted in being sent back to live with my
mother as previously mentioned. I was becoming
internally frustrated and externally disrespectful to my

grandmother and my foster family. While my grandmother loved me, there was little understanding of what was happening inside of me. Even I couldn't seem to get a handle on who I was. All I knew was that I wanted to be like everyone else. I wanted to have boyfriends, work a job and get things, hang out late and talk longer than my curfew allowed, all of which was a contradiction to what my grandmother wanted for and expected of me. I wasn't back at my mother's house more than a few weeks before circumstances would lead to the second suicide attempt I discussed earlier, which ended with me being left at the mental hospital. This all made college definitely appear to be a dream even further removed for me.

When I was released from the hospital and allowed to go back to my grandmother's house a month and a half late into my senior year, the first thing I did was apply to colleges in the hopes that it would allow me the chance to get away from it all. I was accepted to several schools, but I still had no idea how I would get there. Frustrated and angry, I threw everything into a trash bag along with what I thought were my dreams. But then I would dig back through that trash to pull out my acceptance letters, not because I thought I would be attending school, but because for once, I realized that someone saw potential in me and wanted me.

I graduated high school with no idea of how to get to college, no job and an attitude with the world because I felt that nothing good ever happened to me. In a strange turn of events, one of the schools that I had applied to called again with the opportunity to attend and I decided that no matter what, I was going. I made a few calls that led to getting the financial aid I needed to start school. When the spring semester came, I was dropped off at the campus of Virginia State University (VSU) with no idea where I belonged; I didn't even have an assigned dorm room. My cousin who was working as a night manager at a dorm called her dorm director and got permission for me to spend the night until I could talk with someone the next day.

I walked from building to building until I was enrolled in school. When I called to get the rest of my things from my mother, she dropped them off in two trash bags. Once again, I was the trash to be put out and not a daughter or person to be missed. I would sleep on borrowed sheets, study with borrowed books and do everything I could not to go back to live with anyone, especially not my mother. I was 17 years-old and on my own, street-wise and yet still so naïve.

When I first stepped onto the VSU campus, I was in an unknown world that would ultimately be the place where many decisions would be made, both good and bad, as well as serve as the place where I would have to deal with the broken parts of me. I worked two jobs and went to school; my goal was not so much graduation as it was never having to go back to where I had come from. I had not yet learned to understand and appreciate that all things were working together for my good; it didn't feel good, but it would work for my good.

Despite the dire state of my situation, I would have an economics professor who would see potential in me and loan me books for two semesters so that I could complete the class. In exchange for tutoring, a classmate in my summer statistics class would offer me a place to lay my head for the summer when I was one day from being on the street. Likewise, I would be offered the opportunity to work as an orientation leader giving me early access to on campus housing and a few dollars to make up the difference needed to cover the fall semester.

Another professor would see beyond the low moments of performance and demand that I retake a test orally and then the written as if sensing that there was more to me than what met the eye. Temptation would come in the form of unethical offers by those who agreed to "take care" of me, but stubborn independence and a respect for the institution of marriage, regardless of my background, would drive my "no" responses. I was destitute and damaged, but I was not desperate.

My walk with God was not perfect, but there was enough driving force of the word to make me still cry out in prayer and hold on to hope. I would change my church membership while in college and begin my greater journey to knowing God more intimately. It would be years before I could fully appreciate what God had allowed to happen for me, but I would come to truly understand the words of Psalm 139: 8: "Where can I go from Your Spirit? Or where can I flee from Your presence? If I go up to heaven, you are there. If I make my bed in hell, you are there." I would make bad choices and make mistakes, but I would find myself back in the place of looking for the true and living God. Tears would be my companion and pain would be by best friend many days, yet I was (and am) fully convinced that while I was finding my way, God was leading me all along. I went to college to get a degree, but what I would also find the beginning of yet another phase of my deliverance.

Dr. Nikita C. Garris-Watson

Two Master's Degrees, but Still Feeling Stupid and Inadequate

"You cannot be escorted by the belief of inadequacy and get to the destination of excellence..." (Israelmore Ayivor).

There are many who have applauded my academic achievements without understanding the pain of their praise. My first Master's degree was pursued not for the love of the subject, but rather as a part of an agreement for the teaching position I had been blessed to obtain. I was separated from my first husband for the second time and needed to be able to take care of my children. I sat in those graduate classes with students that I saw as more intelligent and capable than I was, but with the understanding that if I failed, my children would suffer the consequences. If I failed, I would lose my teaching job and any opportunity at a better life. So I carried the weight of not only my present situation, but the pain of my past, which was still taunting me. I would replay in my mind over and over the harsh words thrown at me many times in my life: that I was not good enough, not ever going to be anything; that I wouldn't amount to anything; that I would be just like all the other "hood" girls; that there was nothing to me. These words chased me down at night as I slept and haunted me during the day as I pressed onward.

Just like undergrad, I worked a full-time job, grabbed a few part-time jobs, took care of my children and still went to school. There were times when I cried from sheer exhaustion, but I understood that I could not quit. Again, I tried to save my marriage, but even together (we were both in grad school at the same time), there was this feeling of having to compete with him and prove myself to his mother (more on that later). We were living paycheck to paycheck, and the consequences of his adultery were still felt financially.

Despite fighting sickness and the side effects of a bad marriage, I finished my first degree and fell in love with the students and wanted to find a way to do more for those I was teaching. I saw myself in so many of those that sat in the desks before me that I began to believe that if I could make it for them, perhaps they could make it, too. In pursuing a second degree, then, I thought it would bring me peace or even boost my self-esteem, but yet again, I soon found myself looking around wishing that my life were different. I was still not yet satisfied. There was an emotional tug of war happening inside of me as I heard God speaking in one ear and the enemy shouting in the other, but I pressed on. I had to.

Dr. Nikita C. Garris-Watson

First Doctoral Attempt ~ Broken and Never Felt Good Enough Anyway

What happens to a dream deferred?
Does it dry up
Like a raisin in the sun? Or fester like a sore-
And then run?
Does it stink like rotten meat?
Or crust and sugar over—
like a syrupy sweet?
Maybe it just sags like a heavy load.
Or does it explode?
(Langston Hughes)

Sitting in church one Sunday, I had a vision and could see myself in a graduation gown with doctoral stripes walking across a stage. I could vividly see the doctoral bars of those who would shake my hand and confer upon me my degree. Four years later, I would start my first doctoral degree.

With the urging of my then supervisor and the desire to find a way to secure a better position, I applied to a PhD program in the summer of 2003. Fear of failure and feelings of inadequacy still haunted me, however. At every turn, I waited for something to happen that would solidify my feelings. As I submitted my application and entry essay, I was certain that a denial would come and I could embrace my disappointment while confirming my feelings of inadequacy. I would be proven wrong. I stared in stunned silence when I opened my admission packet and read the letter of acceptance to the doctoral program. I hesitated when dialing the number to speak with my advisor, silently believing that after one phone call, they would be able to see through my façade of doctoral aspirations. I was wrong…again. The acceptance was confirmed.

As a part of the introduction to doctoral studies, I had to write a paper. I submitted it and received it back, red ink bleeding all over it from grammatical mistakes; that was the excuse I needed. I was set on quitting the program. However, the professor for the course not only corrected me, but comforted me as if she had sensed my pending decision. Attached to my paper was an email message, which I still have, and in it, she said, "You will make it." She encouraged me to understand that many students would come to terms with the next level of expectations for doctoral study, and they were extremely high, as to be expected; so, reluctantly, I decided to keep trying. Throughout the program, my faith and my fears battled head on, course by course. However, no matter how much I prayed, my belief system was battling with my uncertainty. I knew God, but my faith needed an overhaul.

I had completed my coursework with a 3.98 GPA, passed my comprehensive exams with exemplary remarks from my committee and had worked up to the third chapter of my dissertation when my greatest fear came to fruition. While in school, life didn't stop happening. I had to deal with the fight of adultery and divorce, ministry and pain, sickness and, eventually, homelessness all resulting in having to walk away from the program. I had no more fight left in me and I thought that I was finished with this phase of my life. I was never going to get a doctorate. I still considered myself blessed to have made it that far considering the circumstances, but I was done.

It would take time before I would fully comprehend my role in this outcome. I was living a James 1: 8 existence – being double-minded and unstable in all my ways. I see-sawed between faith and fear with such precision that it had become second nature to me;

my mouth would decree one thing, but my heart would believe another. I would lay at the altar and cry out, but then walk away from the altar and bow out. One moment I wanted to finish, the other moment I wanted to fail as proof that I was right about me. Outwardly, I gave the appearance of one that was making great strides, yet internally, I was swimming in the stench of stagnant waters. The word tells us in Proverbs 23:7 that "as a man thinketh in his heart so is he." My heart needed an overhaul so that my faith could come forward with greater certainty.

Dr. Nikita C. Garris-Watson

Doctorate in Ministry

"Confidence is silent. Insecurities are loud"

(Unknown).

I was done, but God was not. Time and time again, people would prophesy to me about becoming a doctor, or I would show up at various events, and "Dr." would appear boldly before my name. It would be another five years before I would attempt to pursue yet another doctoral program. During this five year gap, people would speak the title of "Dr." over my life and I would respond with tears of agony. My cry to God was consistent: "I don't want to want this. God, don't make me go back. I can't handle another failure." I debated as to whether or not I had heard God every time I would hear that the promise was still for me. I cried many nights because I wanted to just be over that possibility.

With growing frequency, I would encounter numerous people from various walks of life who tried to convince me that I needed to finish what I had started. Ironically, I would help others to reach the goal of completing their doctoral degrees, but I just didn't have it in me to fight that fight again, or so I thought. Having made several transitions in the five years since I abruptly stopped the first PhD program, I would encounter a co-worker that I would later discover was a high school classmate, Dr. Darius Beechaum. I would remember little about our time shared in high school as I was more consumed with pain than with pleasant memories. This co-worker, a pastor, would divinely show up and start conversations with me that often led back to the topic of my incomplete doctoral studies. During one of our many exchanges, he reached inside of his pocket and handed me a picture. There in his hand was my old high school graduation picture that I had signed and given to him over 20 years ago.

As I looked at him with confusion clearly etched on my face, he shared that my picture was one of the few things that had not been destroyed in a house fire that his family had survived several years prior. He was not certain why he had kept the picture all of those years, but he knew in his spirit that it was significant. I heard the Holy Spirit that day whisper in my spirit that like that fire, I had survived what had destroyed many others. I would talk with God intensely throughout that day as I examined my need to do what He had shown me so many years before sitting on the front pew of the church.

Divine providence, for it was certainly not coincidence, would have it that this same co-worker who I had now labeled my "workplace pastor" was the vice-president of a local seminary. While I continued to wrangle with my walk, I would call him and enroll once again for the doctoral journey. As I gathered the necessary paperwork, I would sit before the president of the institution and receive my acceptance to pursue a Doctorate in Ministry. Forging ahead with the same battle going on inside of me – me against the inner me - I would not face this battle alone this time. Paper after paper was submitted, wrapped in prayer and at times bathed in tears of familiarity. This battle was to be won and I would wage war with my faith.

Once again, I would complete my coursework with a 3.99 GPA, finalize my proposal and embark upon the dissertation journey. I would cry out on more than one occasion, "Father give me strength," as I pursued my studies while working full-time, pastoring and doing my part in raising a family. Doubt would be met with determination, frustration would fight against faith, fatigue would be met with fervor and God would send words of encouragement along the way.

A set-back would come at the time of my dissertation defense, but having been in this battle before, I was prepared to handle the enemy and the inner me. Individuals would travel from several directions, some to support me, others to spectate; the pressure to defend was upon my shoulders, but the weight of the final outcome was in the hands of God. I would emerge from that moment not just as a *Doctor*, but more so as a daughter of the King who had been used to destroy generational curses and open the door of access for those around me. As I sat and reflected on the process, God would reveal the greater battle that was at hand, for it was less about me than about those who were connected to me. I had been chosen as a battle axe and weapon of war for the Kingdom, and breaking down walls was not going to be easy. There are still days that I sit and reflect on the process that has brought me to where I am today, but then I think about the words that I read somewhere: "God may change your direction, but never His promises." To God be the glory.

Chapter 6 ~ I Do – I Don't (What's Love Got to do With It)

"4 Love is patient; love is kind; love is not envious or boastful or arrogant 5 or rude. It does not insist on its own way; it is not irritable or resentful; 6 it does not rejoice in wrongdoing, but rejoices in the truth. 7 It bears all things, believes all things, hopes all things, endures all things. 8 Love never ends..." (1 Corinthians 13: 4 – 8 NRSV).

First Love

During the summer before the 11th grade, I met a boy who was a real nice guy; pretty goofy, but nice. I liked him a lot, but his mother did not care for me. I don't know why. Maybe she saw the brokenness in me. The thing is she didn't show it overtly, but rather subliminally. I think she had a misconception about who I was. She was divorced and raising her only child. A momma's boy, here was her son now suddenly diverting much of his attention to me. When she learned we were in many of the same classes, she had his scheduled changed so that we would not have so many classes together. I felt like I was in this tug of war with his mother for his attention.

We dated up through the 11th grade, having gone to the Junior Prom together. I don't fully remember all of why the relationship ended, but it did. We had a few things in common and there were no arguments to speak of. We were both in the band, he gave me a lot of attention and we talked a lot on the phone. What I do know for sure is that I didn't want to be the cause of anyone's trouble with their parents and I had enough rejection from my own mother that I never felt comfortable in his mother's presence. I do know that many times I wanted to tell him about my situation to test his response, but I realized that I had neither the courage nor the words to reveal my secrets to anyone. Years later, I'd learn that I was his "first." I was devastated to discover this fact, almost embarrassed, not because of anything he did wrong, but because of the shame I felt and feeling that he had deserved better. The shame of who I was and what had happened to me left me feeling like I had robbed him – perhaps dirtied him even.

I would go on to have two more high school relationships, but after this break up, things would not be the same for me. I would not let myself get that "close" to anyone again like I had with him. I handled the end of our relationship with caution, despite the pain that I carried. I just never wanted to leave other people scarred like me, so I closed myself off.

Although some people would call what I experienced "puppy love," for me, it was my first real public relationship. Sure, there had been those moments in elementary and middle school where I had "play dated," but that was nothing more than classroom interactions and limited phone calls because my life did not permit or need much more. My teenage years were filled with harmful experiences that tormented me. I couldn't really be me, whomever that was. I had grown up entirely too fast and I couldn't understand his innocence or naivety. Perhaps that is the reason we truly broke up. In the grand scheme of things, I realize that this moment in my life was small, but there would be repeats of mother issues and uncertainties that would rear themselves in other relationships over the years.

Dr. Nikita C. Garris-Watson

College Situations

During the last two weeks of my freshman year in in college, I would encounter a person that would be etched in my life longer than expected and deeper than intended. He would become my long-time lover. When we first started seeing each other, we never intended for it to evolve into more than a one night stand, but it soon did. We became "friends with benefits." He became a constant presence in my life over the next several years, which is ironic because nothing in my life up until that point had ever been stable, and even though this kind of relationship should not have represented stability in my life, it did.

Unhealthy as the overall connection was between us, there was an undercurrent of mutual understanding and support. Conversations were purposely kept light and informal in order to avoid making more of the moments than there should be. The combination of our first physical and then emotional connection was comfortable to me because there were no demands. Instead, there was this unspoken understanding that when we were not with somebody, then we would sleep together. This uncanny connection would eventually become a real friendship as the physical relationship dissolved the closer I grew to God.

Then came an interruption in the form of muscles and a smile. We met the summer of my sophomore year quite by accident. He was older than me; in fact, he was a non-traditional student who had been in the Navy, was working part-time, had his own apartment off campus, but had enrolled in school in the pursuit of greater things for his life. Our interactions started off casual; we were just passing time it appeared, but with greater frequency, I would find myself hanging out at his apartment. At first, it was just a "get to know you" type thing, but then it became a relationship that would last for eight months. I even went home with him one Thanksgiving to spend the night with him and his family. He was from the projects in the heart of Portsmouth, Virginia. The environment was so familiar, it was eerie. Perhaps the hood life in any city has a strange way of becoming home.

What I liked about this relationship was that he was from a broken home, too. He didn't even call his mother "mom." He called her by her first name, so it was almost as if he was just as broken as I was in some ways, so it was acceptable and made me feel okay because here was somebody else coming from nothing trying to make something out of his life. So we spent an inordinate amount of time together when we weren't in classes.

Several months into our relationship, on one of the infrequent nights I was in my dorm room and not at his apartment as he was working the late shift, I called him and told him that I had been invited to go out to eat and he said it was okay for me to go. What he didn't know was who I was going to eat with; he didn't ask me specifically who it was I'd be dining with, so I said I'd be with "an old friend." I didn't think much of it at the moment and little was said by him about it. We had never had issues and didn't discuss our expectations other than the importance of maintaining honesty in the relationship. In my mind, then, the mere fact that I had shared the information was being honest.

Nothing happened between me and my friend that night; we just hung out. When I got back to my room, I called him to let him know that I had returned, sharing who I had been with casually and he snapped on me. I was stunned. He started hollering about what if someone had seen us, what would people think and things of that nature. To me, it was no big deal. This was our only big fight, but we ended our relationship after that because we could not agree on what was acceptable practices versus people's perceptions. One fight and everything was over; a flood of feelings hit me like a tsunami. I had no idea how to process what had happened.

Shortly after to this incident, I joined the Army National Guard. I left soon after our break-up, but while I was gone, I kept in communication with his roommate with whom I was real close to. Away for boot camp, I wrote letters to several people just to keep in touch. When I got back, we would reconnect and he joked with me about disrespecting him by going behind his back and sending letters to his roommate, but not to him. After what had happened, I knew that the joke had more truth to it for him then he was willing to admit. We did get back together later that summer for a little while, but things just weren't the same between us.

In the short time that we were back together, however, I had my first pregnancy scare. The pregnancy test read positive and I was terrified. I had always told myself that I would never have any children out of wedlock; that I would not do what my mother had done. He was not too thrilled with the news either. When I went back to the doctor to determine what was next, there was no pregnancy. My body had aborted it. I was so stressed by the entire situation, my body couldn't take it. He and I would not speak again for years and I never told him the outcome of the situation. I figured he was content with the fact that there was no child and I made up my mind that there had never been any real love between us in the first place. Anger soon replaced the hurt and love, fueling feelings of bitterness. The lack of maturity on my part on only saw my side of the situation and I refused to realize that I carried a portion of the burden for what had transpired.

Miscarrying was a relief. Although I had been on the pill since I was 13 years-old due to ongoing problems with my menstrual cycle and concerns with results of pelvic exams, I had not been taking them consistently when I was with him. It was a stupid choice on my part, but I had always assumed that I could not have children. The doctors had convinced my grandmother to put me on the pill because of these health issues. When I look back on it, I believe it all had something to do with having been violated so young. As recently as 2016, my GYN mentioned that I had a lot of scar tissue in my reproductive cavity.

One of the big things I learned from this relationship is that perception is important to men; in his case, it was partially about control, but more so, it was about the mutual respect that both parties deserved. I was not completely open with him that night and the consequence was the loss of the relationship. I would take with me a lot more lessons from that relationship, such as good can help to make you great and bad can help to make you better if you are willing to learn from your mistakes.

Although I had my issues, I was not okay with leaving someone in pain. I had come to realize some objectionable things about myself in that relationship, so I began to pay closer attention to each interaction or relationship I encountered, no matter how brief it was; it became a study in self. I didn't always like what I saw about me and there were times I was quick to place blame, but ultimately, I had to face me. As I grew in God, I would find myself praying for those I had crossed in my walk during my brokenness. Not just for my part in their lives, but also for their healing and, ultimately, happiness.

Dr. Nikita C. Garris-Watson

My First Marriage

*"When something bad happens, you have three choices.
You can either let it define you, let it destroy you, or let
it strengthen you" (Unknown).*

Prior to my first marriage, I rarely fought to save any relationships as I have previously mentioned. I accepted failure as part of the process and ultimately as the way it would simply be. Rejection played a major role in my thinking and pain was so familiar that it almost became the acceptable norm.

I met my first husband on the college campus of Virginia State University. He was a first year graduate student at the time and it was my last year as an undergrad. I had recently ended the previously discussed relationship and really wasn't looking to be involved with anyone. He was standing outside of Singleton Hall, which was the business department, talking to a few students. I was going into the bookstore when I saw him. I was with a friend and I remember looking at him and telling my friend, "I think I'll make him mine." We both laughed out loud and kept walking. It was merely a fly by night comment with no intended follow through, so I didn't stop or say anything to him.

I found out later on that he had seen me at the same moment I saw him and had followed me into the bookstore; he had come in and asked a fellow student, his frat brother, who I was because he had seen me talking to him as I made my way into the door. We were then introduced and started a polite conversation. We would later exchange numbers and a few days later find ourselves talking about a little bit of everything. I talked, but I also listened intently.

Dr. Nikita C. Garris-Watson

Here was this clean cut man who had a degree, was a military officer and came from a two-parent home, although his father was deceased. I would sit and wonder what we could possibly have in common, and I thought perhaps if I told him only surface things about me, there would be no room for the truth to be exposed. Conversely, part of me was so tired of hiding my truths that I wanted to tell him everything about me and then see what the outcome would be. Rejection would be nothing new, and disgust I saw every day when I looked in the mirror. Of course, I said nothing. I tried to enjoy our time together, but my own life seemed to be pressing on the back of my mind with greater intensity. One night on a drive to the store, one question from him forced me to tell him more about my life than I had ever intended. I would attempt to skillfully share only what was comfortable while presenting the "Reader's Digest" version of my story.

Despite what I had shared, the relationship continued to progress; was it his curiosity or was he crazy, I wondered to myself? We were soon in the sixth month window and we were getting along wonderfully. Marriage was the furthest thing from my mind. I only assumed that some of his "pedigree" would rub off on me during our relationship. However, we would get married after only eight months of dating. In my mind, I thought that if I didn't marry him, then I would lose the "good" boy and my chance of solidifying my "new" identity. It wasn't that I didn't love him, but nothing about me was ready to be married or a wife. What I would come to understand years later into the marriage was that I married this man for the wrong reasons. I wanted him to make me clean or make me feel beautiful. I wanted him to fix all of my feelings of inadequacy and inferiority. I wanted him to do all of that for me. I wanted him to be the perfect man, but he couldn't be. No one can. But I figured that if he was going to marry me, then he was going to do all of those things for me: fix the rejection and low self-esteem.

In hindsight, I realize that I did not even consider what contribution I was going to bring to the marriage because I didn't think I had anything to offer equally. I was just going to be the trophy wife, and I don't mean in terms of not working because I had always worked and planned to continue to do so. But what I wanted was for his perceived greatness to define my greatness, and that was my mistake. I would walk into this marriage anticipating a happily-ever-after Cinderella story, but before it was over, find myself in the middle of 'Nightmare on Elm Street.'

Had I paid attention or had wisdom, I would have fully realized before we even got married that none of this was going to work out in my favor, especially after I met his mother. That was probably one of the worst experiences of my life. I learned quickly into the marriage that he was also a momma's boy. This was a major red flag. God gives us plenty of red flags, but like many people, I refused to see them truly because I was never taught to look for them, let alone what they even were. More so, my flesh wanted what my flesh wanted.

My first husband was the youngest of five children having been his mother's last child at age 40. So he was truly spoiled. He could not make a move in his life, I'd soon learn, without her input or approval. Parental respect and appreciation is by far important and should be applauded, however, there is a leave and cleave that comes with marriage that cannot be obtained when relationships are out of balance.

During my initial visit with her, I brought her flowers and sorority gifts to try and present the best image, making every effort to be as polite and as articulate as I could. In response, I would be quickly informed that he had just ended a long-term relationship with a woman that she adored, and she made it clear that

Dr. Nikita C. Garris-Watson

I was never going to be *her*. His mother had her heart set on the *other* woman, and time would show me that he, too, was not ready to move past what once was. Again, I was not good enough for another woman's son. However, instead of walking away from this relationship, I told myself that I was not dating her and wouldn't have to see her often, so what she thought about me should not matter.

The second red flag involved an affair that he had with another woman while in the relationship with said woman before me. A child was produced out of that situation and was given his last name. He would find out during delivery that the child was not his, but he never cleared up the matter of that child having his last name. This situation would be revealed only because of a conversation I overheard while he was on the phone. This person would be the reason for our first fight and over the years, she would be in the marriage just as much as I was.

After our marriage, as angry as I would become behind the frequent adulterous interactions between the two of them, I would hurt most for the little girl that had a last name and no father to whom to connect. Selfishly and repeatedly, I had initially demanded that her name be properly changed to reflect her true biological father's last name convinced that this mistake was robbing me and my children of some rite of passage. As God dealt with my heart, I realized that her suffering far outweighed the pride of a last name. Still, I would view her birth certificate for proof of her biological history and then become enraged that her parents would leave her in the awkward positon of having a name to which she had no true blood connection. I was a walking oxymoron! I wanted to fight for the rights of a child to whom I had no responsibility, yet at the same time, I wanted to fight the mother of this same child for her repeated intrusion into my marriage.

Dr. Nikita C. Garris-Watson

So all of these red flags are waving in the wind like kites on a cool breeze, but I didn't take heed. As far as I was concerned at the time, he was a good man and he was going to make me great. He had one degree and was now pursuing a Master's in psychology; he had a car, he taught me how to drive a stick shift and he was a 1st Lieutenant in the reserves. Heck, my grandmother even liked him because she thought he was so respectful.

One of the things that I first admired about my husband would soon become one of the things that frustrated me the most about being in his life. His studies in psychologically shifted me from a lover on equal footing to a field rat in the classroom of life. I was more his psychological experiment than his girlfriend (and later his wife). He would use me for all of his classes. I was his case study. So I began to feel more like his "client" than the love of his life. His hero syndrome had him looking at all of my dysfunctions and thinking that he could fix and then save me, or at best, "treat" me unofficially.

I became pregnant with our son, our first child, a month and two weeks after we got married. Both of us were caught off guard by the pregnancy having made plans to wait three years before introducing children into our lives. Although we had not abstained prior to marriage, I was convinced based on previous doctors' reports that I would never be able to have children and if I did, it would require medical intervention. Despite the previous miscarriage, I and the doctors were convinced it had been a fluke that would not easily be repeated.

In keeping with his military commitment, my husband would leave for a few weeks out of the year for training in the reserves. When I was four months pregnant, he left to go on assignment and I was left to move us from a one bedroom apartment to a three bedroom apartment in preparation for the arrival of the baby. One night, I awoke to a strong pain. I felt a rip tear through my spirit. I knew right then and there that something was horribly wrong and was sure my husband had cheated on me. I tried to convince myself that it was just me, that I was being overly sensitive and that the pain was the result of the previous day's strenuous activity. But almost immediately after that night, his phone calls to house become less frequent. In fact, it would be four days from that night before I would hear from him and that is only because I had to track him down on base to get information from him. When I spoke with him, he was extremely evasive and distant in his response. Again, I took responsibility and excused his behavior claiming that I was tired or even missing him and overreacting to what I was hearing.

When he finally returned home from the assignment and walked through the front door, I was excited to see him, but I could tell that something was not right, but again, I ignored my feelings. We slept together that night. After nearly three, almost four weeks away from one another, it would have been impossible to avoid. A few days later, I was not feeling right. I was itching and feeling horrible. Experiencing a high risk pregnancy, I was keenly aware of every change in my body.

He tried to give me what he said were vitamins, but I soon learned that it was the medication he had been given to clear up the STD he had contracted from his affair while away. Instead of coming home and telling me what happened, and choosing not to sleep with me to protect us, he kept it to himself until he could no longer do so. The pain from what I was experiencing in my body finally made him come clean and tell me everything. I was devastated; this was not supposed to happen. He was supposed to be the good guy, the perfect man. Despite my suspicion, I was, for the first time, ready to be wrong about what I thought I knew. The next day after his confession, I made him call my doctor and tell him what he had done because I was too embarrassed and humiliated. I was so broken. I was diagnosed with an STD while pregnant with our first child.

I went from loving him with everything in me to hating him within a matter of months into the marriage. I was literally broken, but I was also so angry that I wanted to kill both him and the woman he had slept with. As if to provoke my pain, the woman he had the affair with started calling my house and hanging up when I would answer. In addition to this South Carolina mistress, I then discovered that he was still having a relationship with the mother of the child he had learned was not his. It was all so much; he had not protected any of us. The range of emotions were more than I could handle.

I contemplated packing up and leaving, but then I started thinking about the fact that my son would not have a father. The thought that I would bring a child, a son, into the world without a father was more weight than the pain of being betrayed. I could not allow the unborn child that I was carrying to come into the world and suffer the feelings that I was faced with daily. I didn't want to fulfill the idea of being another single mother raising a son without a father. I battled with myself night and day as I fought between staying and going. I was too far along to have an abortion, and despite the unplanned arrival, I had fallen in love with the child I was carrying. I was so proud that my child and I shared the same last name as the father, yet I was so hurt that there were moments where I couldn't breathe. Fresh wounds would mate with old wounds producing a new bitterness in me that would take more years than expected to heal from. In the end, I decided to stay; in hindsight, I realize that I should have left then. Not only did I stay, but the two main mistresses stayed as well as others who would join in the ranks. As I stated before, the one he had dated before me, who claimed her child was his and it was not, was pretty much in the marriage for as long as I was in the marriage

The drama that was my first marriage went on for years. Sometimes, a little information can be *a lot* dangerous. I became a pseudo detective snooping into everything, and finding something with every twist and turn. It was too much. When we finally separated, I had no intentions of going back to him. I had even started seeing someone else and had also decided that I was never going to get married to anyone ever again. But then one night, we got together during a moment of weakness, and I became pregnant with our daughter. The flesh had won again. I felt so trapped. This was my third pregnancy by my husband, including the one after the birth of my son that had ended in a miscarriage, which I never bothered to tell him about because I was more relieved than hurt. Yet, here I was with two children now, working three jobs while going to school for a graduate degree, and feeling as though I was losing myself in all of it.

Reluctantly, we decided to get back together in an effort to spiritualize our relationship. We went to several different counselors. We went to one pastor whom we later discovered was cheating on *his* wife. It was all a waste of time because I realized that I had actually not forgiven him in order for us to truly start over. I was always looking and waiting for the next thing. And the bad part about always looking for that next thing, is that you do end up finding it.

The best counselor during that time would end up being God and the alone time where He made me face me. I did not instantly respond, and I was always ready to defend myself, but God was relentless in pursuing the deeper portions of me that needed healing. I would fight the process because it was too painful to deal with my past and present realities. Life refused to be still and hurt continued to pile on before I could find healing or stability. I stayed on the defense looking for the next piece of proof to validate my anger and fuel my frustration. My mouth was saying I wanted to be healed, but my actions were building a case against me. I was the victim and in my warped thinking, he was now in debt to me. The only acceptable payment was for him to suffer, so therefore, every argument was crafted to remind him of what he had done to me. Like a skilled historian, I would recall every detail of every incident that had taken place. But the more I fought him, the more I was forced to confront my brokenness and bitterness face-to-face, much of it present long before he had entered into my life.

I was so angry and had begun to comprise myself on another level. Instead of being angry about the violations of the institution of marriage, I allowed my low self-esteem to begin speaking for me. My comments became: If you are going to cheat, then at least leave the house in good standing; If you are going to cheat, then at least be honest with me; If you are going to cheat, the least you could do is make sure to take care of me financially. After all, we were struggling. I was working two or three jobs, barely making it. So I was angry because, well, why couldn't I be a "kept" woman, I thought? He was taking care of everyone other woman *except* for me.

Seven years into the marriage, I made the horrific decision to get even. I thought, "Well, two can play this game and if I play it, I'm gonna play it better than you." So the thing I had promised myself I'd never do, I did. I had enough proof to fuel my pain, and enough pain to rationalize my plot. I cheated on my husband twice: one affair lasted a week and the other a couple of months. The thing is that when you do something to hurt someone else, you ultimately discover that you are really only hurting yourself. After everything exploded, when I looked in the mirror, I saw a nasty foul woman staring back at me. Unlike the violations of my past, I had *chosen* this path, and I would find it harder to recover from my own violations of the marriage than I would his repeated offenses.

I couldn't pretend that I didn't know what I was doing was wrong; I knew and I did it anyway. I couldn't hide behind the excuse of pain, for that would only work for a moment before I would feel the conviction of going against everything that I stood for. What I thought would make me feel better, left me more broken than before. I would drag myself to church over and over looking for healing. The altar would become my weekly visitation as I fought to find a way out of the old and new pain that gripped me equally. Just like Adam and Eve, I would try to hide from God hoping that He would just go away and leave me alone. I hated my life and all that it had come to represent. I felt like a walking contradiction wanting to be healed, yet wanting to hold onto my pain.

I tried many times to use sex to fix the problems in our marriage, thinking I could make everyone else go away, but I soon learned that the moments were not being fixed. I was simply putting a band-aid on a bullet wound. However, because of my strong belief that children need a father in their lives, maintaining what I saw as a whole house for my kids became priority as I alluded to earlier; however, whole and healthy are not necessarily synonymous. When I discovered that I was having a baby girl, for instance, I was adamant that she know her father even after I realized that the marriage was not going to work. This same belief forced me to stay longer in the marriage than I should have, but it was so important to me to give my children something that I never had: a last name and a person to associate it with other than me. I didn't want them to be damaged like me. In the end, though, staying *did* damage them anyway because they heard the fights and yelling from our arguments.

Dr. Nikita C. Garris-Watson

I would ride the rollercoaster that was my first marriage for 14 years. Although we had left each other four times over the course of the marriage, we always came back to one another, and each time, the fall out would be worse. We would have these few months of peace and then it would be something or somebody else. The relationship was toxic. There was never a sense of everything was going to be okay. I lived in constant fear and torment every time we would get together, waiting for the next problem to surface. I could find no peace. Every time he left the house, I was certain it was to cheat. Even if he was trying to make it better, the atmosphere of the home was not conducive for healing because constantly hanging over his head were the accusations of adultery. Where he could once do no wrong in my eyes, he could now do no right. The word tells us in Proverbs 21:9: "It is better to dwell in a corner of the housetop, than with a brawling woman in a wide house." I am sure that I made him seek the rooftop on many days.

But God would not give room to my pity parties, and during these days of torment, I would encounter those who challenged me in the spirit and in the natural. Helplessly, I would prostrate myself before Him trying to hear God's voice for direction. I knew there had to be more to life than what I had experienced at that point and I needed to find out what it was for me. I would dredge through days like a zombie keeping up appearances, but living in agony. Intercessory prayer at the church would be my comfort and combat zone as I fought for my life with each moment. Depression was available in daily doses and I should have overdosed on my intake of it, but I had learned how to be functionally dysfunctional. The greatest challenge was not the preached word, for I had learned to hear and not hear, but the one-on-one moments when God would send someone to spiritually confront me, did not allow me to escape so easily. I would find a secondary intercessory prayer group, called

House of Prayer, held by one of the women in our church. I didn't know it then, but House of Prayer would become my House of Hope and Healing as God dealt with the inside of me.

People often blame God and others for their bad decisions, but the truth of the matter is that we were both in church during this tumultuous time. However, we were not allowing God to genuinely deal with either one of us. I remember crying out to God often about our marriage and my past, but when God would show me myself, I would play the victim. God was not ignoring my hurt. God was showing me all of my hurt so that I could heal, but I had spent more time pointing fingers at those around me than I did dealing with me.

I could have been healed sooner had I been willing to deal with myself; instead, I was too busy trying to pinpoint the wrongs of those who had mistreated me and mishandled me. I was living a James 1:8 amplified version life: "double-minded and unstable in all my ways." Even in the midst of my fight, God was dealing with the real me. I distinctly remember going to the bookstore and grabbing a book called, *Tough Talk to a Stubborn Spouse*, by Stephen Schwanbach, thinking I would read it and deal with my husband. Little did I know how much that book would slap me in the face breaking down my stubborn resistance.

Ironically, as time would pass, I would end up literally ministering to a few of his mistresses. And when I say minister, I mean I prayed for and labored with them in person and over the phone. Despite my own hurt, I would come to understand their brokenness – seeking the face of God for the answers to why they would enter into an adulterous relationship knowingly. It would take a great dose of God's spirit and love to cause me to understand why they were so fractured, and pray and minister and pour into their broken places even while I was still healing.

That takes a whole lot of God. You want to cut somebody, but God says cover them in prayer. You want to lash out, but God says love them. Give them the God-love. It took all of God in me to do this, but because of who I was destined to be in ministry – who He was developing me to be at that time – I could feel their pain. He did not allow me to NOT feel it. In some regard, they were just as much victims as I was. Not because they were innocent of their participation, but they had shared personal pains that were used to draw them in and hold them hostage. Although I did not see it that way in the beginning because I thought they were villains, God showed me the victims in them that had also been manipulated, taken for granted and abused. He made me see even the genesis of their problems when I didn't want to see it, but I had to because it would make me a better person.

Dr. Nikita C. Garris-Watson

Called to Preach in the Midst of the Valley

"18 The Spirit of the Lord is upon me, because he hath anointed me to preach the gospel to the poor; he hath sent me to heal the brokenhearted, to preach deliverance to the captives, and recovering of sight to the blind, to set at liberty them that are bruised" (Luke 4:18).

Getting saved and living saved required levels of dependence on God that would challenge me to change daily. I would discover that finding faith and stabilizing my spiritual walk would be the greatest on-going battle of my life. The enemy would fight me on the outside as I fought with me on the inside. Having lived daily with dysfunction for so long, there were certain behaviors and mindsets which had become norms. Although I could not deny the life that I had been subjected to, I also could not willingly allow my past to set the tone or pace for my pursuit of God. Despite the desire on many occasions to sit down and quit life, there was nothing to be gained from those moments. Outside of the basics of belief in God and His ability to save, there is not a one-size fits all prescription for living the life of a believer.

I would spend years being purged and purified, going through monumental moments of deliverance and then falling on my face in failure. For instance, I was standing in church one Sunday and internally I said to God, "I quit! I cannot live the life that you expect of me. I cannot maintain this standard of holiness that is required. I am going to keep failing you, so this is my last day trying to live holy." The very next moment, the preacher stood up and preached a message entitled, "Don't Give Up!" His introduction grasped my heart strings with such force that I knew in that moment God had heard me and was speaking directly to *me*.

For years, it seemed that being saved was either going to take my fight away from me or it was not all that others made it appear to be. The highs and lows of life threatened to pull me back into what I knew where attitudes and actions that were unacceptable to God. I would read the *Bible* in frustration trying to find out how to get to the blessing only to have to learn that until the lesson is learned, the true blessing cannot be received. There were opportunities that God wanted me to have, but I would be my own greatest obstacle. Yes, I would blame people and problems, but internally, I knew that I was responsible for deciding the level of control that I permitted any of these outside influences to have on me. As Maya Angelou stated, "I did then what I knew how to do. Now that I know better, I do better." Little by little, I was learning better and *better* was being required of me.

The word tells us in Hebrews 11:1 that "now faith is the substance of things hoped for the evidence of things not seen." I would fight to find the faith for now and later. Having grown up with so many disappointments and unfulfilled expectations, I wavered between expecting only the worst and expecting nothing so that I could not be disappointed. It would take several encounters with God to modify my mindset and walk in the place of supernatural faith. He would allow me to endure what felt like painstaking tests only to fine tune my spiritual hearing and eyesight. It is important to note, that most of these tests where the end results of doing it my way and having to face the Self-Inflicting Nonsense (SIN) consequences. I admit trying to use lazy loopholes to avoid responsibility, including using the "church is full of hypocrites" excuse only to have God strongly respond with the challenge to be the change that I wanted to see. It seemed unfair that God would have such high standards set for me when clearly I had what I deemed good excuses for my ways. Ultimately, my journey would teach me that I was called to be an example, not to live with excuses.

You never know when God will call you to serve. In fact, I did not ever think that I had a call on my life or even knew that is was possible for someone like me to have an assignment in the Kingdom of God. I was working on simply being and living saved. Even though my life, mind and marriage were a mess, once I got saved, I never really stopped going to church. My consistency in attendance would increase even as I fought with an inconsistent lifestyle. I was still longing to know God and solidify my relationship with Him.

However, I just could not rectify the two desires raging inside of me: to know God and to want revenge, which resulted in living in sin. I was torn in half. The hard part of it all was that you do run into hypocritical people in the church and I did that, and was even one myself for a while. There were some folks in the church who believed that it was okay to lead the double life that I was leading, but it was not. I even had preachers who would approach me. They would preach to me and then prey on me, but I could not make peace with that and it was in those times that I would temporarily withdraw from the church in confusion. Nonetheless, there was still this longing to get right and stay right, and that was tugging at my soul mercilessly. You can leave the church and Christ will still pursue you, for indeed, He is truly married to the backslider (Jerimiah 3:14).

As situations and circumstances would happen, the tug of war on my soul would only increase even more so after I had cheated twice on my husband. I could not deal with the consequences of how I felt. The feelings were so close to how I felt when I had been molested: that same dirty, broken feeling. And although I could fight over my reasons for why I had cheated, I could not rationalize it with my faith. Oh, I tried to, though. I'd say things like, "Well, God, he's doing this, he's not doing that." I would debate with God about why my husband could do what he wanted, but I couldn't. "Why do I have to be the one to keep giving and praying?" I got angry because I had felt like that all of my life: I've had to take what was being done to me. And at one point during all of this, I felt like the church was not helping me. It was not healing the broken places; it wasn't getting to the depths of my pain. Here I am in church shouting and praising Him, but I am still not yet healed from my past and enduring the pains of my then present.

All of this is playing out at the same time: the broken marriage, the battle to live right and the prophecies that were coming with increasing frequency that there was a call on my life. I was plagued with the question of who am I not just spiritually, but literally, "Why am I here? Why is God keeping me alive?" I remember wanting to die, but I couldn't because I had these two babies. If I were to die, then they'd be left with all of the mess and chaos. I often believe that God gave me my children to save my life, and not because I was so great of a parent, but because of my love for Sasha and Steven, there were choices that I simply could not and would not make, and these decisions *saved* my life. For a season, living for them was the only reason I existed. If they had not been present during this portion of my life, I can honestly say that I don't know what I would have done.

Luke 4:18 is the scripture I have come to lean on and would be the scripture that God would use to call me into ministry. It came to me at a time when I was most broken, most battered and bruised. People had been telling me for years that I was called to preach. I would rebuke them without hesitation, informing them that they had *misunderstood God* and that there was no way possible I was called to preach. By this time, my husband had already been preaching and there were only temporary changes in his behavior before the affairs and lies would start yet again. I decided that if I was going to be a hypocrite, I was not going to be one in the pulpit.

The truth is, I did not see myself as having spiritual worth or value. All I could see was every mistake I had made, and so I thought that I dared not step into anyone's pulpit. I was not worthy or clean. I was the least of the least. I had not grown up in church, yet it seems like it was always in my broken places – moments – where I would seek after God. I would have these experiences and encounters with Him when I was the most broken that would leave me with internal changes that could not be denied. In short, God would not let me die. My spiritual steps were growing increasingly steady and strong, but my self-esteem was battered and torn. I had committed myself to finding God for myself and would find Him in the most unusual times and places.

A member of a large congregation of believers, I discovered a core group of power that I had not known existed in our walls - the Tuesday night intercessory group. This small population of prayer warriors seated within the large scale group of parishioners was phenomenal. I would join their ranks weekly and learn the art and war of prayer, drinking spiritual knowledge that has been with me ever since. I would change my class schedule and work schedule so as not to miss this weekly encounter with God. I knew there was more to them than what met the eye and I would be privileged to learn that they not only met faithfully in the church, but had a rotating schedule outside of the church. Like a prayer junkie, I would find every opportunity to be in their presence and learn more about God.

As my prayer life grew, so did my persistence in pursuing the things of God. I would devour books, attend conferences and search out classes that would give me information about being a believer. I would find myself as an almost permanent fixture at the altar fighting layers of my life with each turn. The church would begin holding once a month evening healing and deliverance services and I would attend loyally seeking to find my way out of many things and getting into the presence of God. During one such service, I encountered the person who would become my first and consistent spiritual mother.

As I laid at the edge of the altar, a puddle of tears and agony, she sat down next to me and prayed for me with such fervency. Standing under five feet tall, I had only seen her a few times in church, but clearly, she was a giant in the spirit. From that day forward, I called her my "Reverend Mother," a title that has not changed in over 25 years. There would be seasons I would see her almost daily and then seasons of infrequent visibility, but I would find a comfort in our relationship that I had not known with anyone other than my grandmother. At her feet, I would gain wisdom about God and spiritual warfare that would shape my ministry. Often more than not, I would lay on her floor and deal with yet another moment that had haunted my life. A discerning woman, there was no being comfortable with sin, for she would identify and confront any unconfessed or hidden issues of the heart. I had never been handled so thoroughly and yet so tenderly in my entire life. Where others avoided her when they didn't want to be accountable, I, on the other hand, ran to her for accountability in keeping me from becoming complacent in my spirituality. God knew what I needed and He was strategically lining it all up to get the best out of me.

Oddly enough, the husband I was battling to not hate was one of the main people telling me that I was called to preach. In fact, he convinced me to go and talk with our then pastor about it. However, the bigger issue was also that the church I was attending did not license women to preach at that time. So there were no women preachers *anywhere* in the church. Over the years, I had watched those with obvious callings subdue what they felt and others confront it and then leave in frustration. Thus, for me, being called to preach was a spiritual death sentence because I felt like I was not going to fit in again. I did not grow up in the church, as I mentioned before, so who was I going to talk to? No one in my family had been preachers; heck, no one in my biological family was even saved that I knew of! It was going to be controversial and I was still struggling with who I was.

Sixteen years into my spiritual journey, 11 of them spent at this church, I finally decided to go and talk with the pastor. I was gaining a certainty of the call and rest was no longer accessible to me as I had spent what was now three years knowing what was being asked of me. I could not get rid of the truth of what I was being asked to do. So I went to speak with him, but my husband would not go with me. He told me that I was called, yet he did not go with me to the most monumental moment in my spiritual walk and life. By now, I was so used to being in this relationship were I had to protect myself from everything, I was not at all surprised that he did not go with me. However, I felt that if he had gone with me that first time, it would have given me a sense of strength. That moment of loneliness would prepare me for many other major ministry walks that I would encounter in my spiritual journey, and my testimony would be that seasons of separation and elevation often come hand in hand.

I met with the pastor. I had my whole theological argument prepared, and what was so interesting was that before we prayed, he told me that God had already told him why I was coming to see him. After praying, and after I presented my case, the only thing he said was that it was not his preference to license women. How does one argue against someone's preference? How do you argue with a man about his opinion when this is his church? And how can you tell me that God had already told you I was coming and then tell me that it is not *your* preference to license women to preach? Why not tell me what God said? Still, I had to give the pastor credit for that moment; while he stood his ground, he never stated that I was *not* called. Over the years as I replayed that day in my mind, I would remember most of all not *what* he said, but what he did *not* say.

I was so frustrated and confused when I left his office that day. The meeting left me feeling rejected, abandoned and uncovered. It was as if another father had denied my paternity and I was left empty. People use the term "spiritual father," and for me, in that moment of my life, here I was again - twice - with no father. No father in my *natural* life and no father in the *spirit/gospel*. In the natural, a father is supposed to guide you - lead you, establishing standards for behavior and serving as the example for which his children base expectations. In the *Bible*, fathers would help their offspring to come into the place of identity, pronouncing blessings that would come and the associated responsibilities. How was I supposed to preach without a license – go forth in ministry without a father? I had nobody.

Conversely, while the pastor had just told me that it was not his preference to license women, on my subsequent visit to him (yes, I went back to ask questions), he gave me permission to take certain assignments and go to classes. But what was the point, I thought? Or maybe I had misunderstood God completely and needed to accept that fact. Again, I was stuck with no clue as to where to go or what to do next.

Not more than three months after my initial meeting with the pastor, I was asked to preach at small church. It was as if God was re-emphasizing that He had called me to preach. I would reluctantly take the assignment, but six months later, I went back to the pastor. He told me at *this* meeting that he could see himself eventually licensing women and he talked about key women in his life who had been influential to his ministry, but again, he didn't know when he, himself, could license one to preach. I asked him what I was supposed to do because I felt like a bastard. I was taking classes and doing things here and there, but I was not licensed.

So I asked God what to do. I started going to different conferences and classes where I knew no one, but everywhere I went, people would repeat over and over, 'you are called to preach; you have been chosen to lead.' But instead of finding joy in the words being spoken over my life, I would get angry because they were asking me to do something that I thought I could not do. How was I just going to preach? Which direction was I supposed to take? How could I preach when I had no one to help me? The words would be agony to my spirit as I wrestled for answers that I could not go to my leader, my husband or anyone that I could identify to help me understand.

I went back to the pastor for a third time about two and a half years later and expressed my feelings to him. He told me to consider leaving the church because I could not continue to function effectively the way that I was feeling. He recommended that I leave the church for a year, and that if I took his advice and left, but came back before then, I would not be able to stay away. That was not the answer I neither expected nor wanted to hear. I talked to my then husband about it. He was on the ministerial staff at that time. I told him that I had not asked the pastor to leave. I just didn't know how to stay. I decided after that not to "do" church anymore. I was called, but now I was more confused than ever about my next step. I would visit different churches and periodically attended conferences just to keep my spirits up because I needed something. My faith had taken a beating, and just like previously in life, I had told my truth and was rejected and abandoned. I didn't know who to trust because it had been broken, all my life, in fact. So there I was. Transition was upon me, but my trust issues were crippling and haunting me as I tried to find my next spiritual place.

But God is amazing. He will always bring you to the place where you need to be. Prior to leaving my church, I was blessed to have met a woman who would become instrumental in my training; a power house preacher, I would attend her Joy In the Morning Ministries Conference and come across yet another young female preacher who would meet me at the altar stating that, "God said with all the hell you've been through, you don't have a right to shut your mouth." This woman who is an international preacher today, did not know me from Adam, but what she said broke me so much in that moment. As I crumbled to the floor, she joined me speaking words that would cause me to confront the very essence of who I was. God's words through her would demand that I deal with myself and the demons that haunted me. But what good am I to the Kingdom, I thought? I never felt my life was valuable or usable. It was that experience with those two women that made me sit still long enough to really hear God's voice

After searching for my safe place to worship, I would eventually find the church where it would all come together. Serving under a seasoned leader who had left the traditional church to start his own ministry, I walked in the door not asking to preach. In fact, my first words when I decided to join his church were, "What can I do and where can I best serve?" He would observe me, making insightful observations as I would make an effort to show up early and stay late to help. Wearing stilettos while cleaning with a scrub brush was not beneath me, for I was certain that I had found my resting place and would give my best. My pastor would say something to me about the "call" on my life, though I had intentions on keeping it to myself. I was convinced that I could "appease" God by being busy in the church.

Ministry training would not be easy, for *this* pastor was a preacher's preacher and the standards would be set high, seemingly at moments even higher for me. Stepping into the pulpit would be no easy journey and sermons would be preached in front of him first with great scrutiny. Although intimidating, the training was preparing me. With his permission, in addition to the intense schedule of our ministry, I would drive three hours one way every week to attend a ministerial school that would stretch me tremendously. In the midst, I would learn the ministry of transparency; my brokenness is what I use to help people hold onto God. I wept then and I sometimes still weep because it still doesn't make sense to me at moments that God could take such misery and birth ministry.

As I was finding my place in God, I was still fighting how to handle what was happening right in my own home. As I stated before, my then husband and I had separated four times before finally ending the marriage for good. We were both evolving, but not together and not both towards God. The call on my life had been tested to the limits after being thrust into the role of ministering to his lovers, but after trying to pray it through and be spiritual about it, I got to a place where I could not take it anymore. After 14 years of fighting back and forth, and going through cycles, we were through. I wanted a healthy house, and I did not have that. I also realized that I did not love him anymore. I was healing from my past while dealing with the pain of my present and a decision had to be made. I was convinced that he had never loved me and that we were only causing each other more pain by staying together. There are those who would debate the theology of divorce, yet God was not required to hold together what neither of us had sought his wisdom for before entering into the relationship. My ex-husband was and still is not a bad person, but neither of us were prepared to be married, nor to meet the needs of the other party. Neither of us needed to be married until we had dealt with the internal issues that would surface with each situation that arose within the marriage.

Being called to preach in the midst of my valley was the ultimate conflict of my life because it didn't make sense. It was not a euphoric feeling. My greatest burden would also be my greatest blessing. My path to ministry was unorthodox, but it was mine to walk. This walk had left me with *infallible proof* - my own experiences that could not be disputed or refuted. As the mothers in the church would say, "I know too much about Him and you can't make me doubt Him. I know that I know that I know." I would find great struggles and success along the way, but God allowed me to learn more and more about Him and His plan for me. The journey would include those who would embrace me and those who would reject me, and each group would force me to go back to God. As I cautiously took steps towards my destiny, I would seek after God harder than anything that I had ever sought for in my life. The altar would be the place that God would alter the deepest places in me bringing about healing that could only be found in His presence.

Dr. Nikita C. Garris-Watson

Homeless with Children

"Hardships often prepare people for an extraordinary destiny" (CS Lewis).

My marriage was finally over. I had finally come to the point where I knew I was not going to try and continue to "save" the marriage. Upon ending it, however, I had learned that there was no money for me and our children because he had put it all in a joint account with his mistress. The bills were not being paid consistently because I was trying to now do it all by myself. The mortgage was behind and I was tired. I would normally have tried to buckle down and take care of everything, but, again, I had no more fight in me. At this same time, I discovered a lump in my breast after going to the doctor. So here I was divorcing, while agonizing over the lump in my breast, which would eventually require surgery, and I was still facing other health issues requiring treatment that was constantly being adjusted.

I finally decided that I could not hold it together anymore, and I gave in. We lost the house. The kids and I ended up being homeless. I put our stuff in storage and was able to rent a room. We now lived in one room with a mattress on the floor. My son was in the 8th grade and my daughter in the 5th. At the time, I was still working on the first doctoral program discussed earlier, but as stated, I would later have to drop out after completing the third chapter of my dissertation following my divorce.

With the divorce in progress, a new routine ensued; I would get the kids dressed, drop them off at each of their schools, go to work, and then pick them up, feed them and then we'd just pray together. This was our life every day for months. The laundromat became an outing and the car became our playground. We had nothing, but we did have each other.

Now, I thought I was keeping this secret from every one. I had not told anyone what was really going on in our lives, not even my sister whom I was fairly close to. The new church that we were attending was none the wiser as we all stayed at the same church for two years before anyone other than the pastors knew that we were divorcing. Yet, even the leaders had no idea how bad the situation *really* was. That all soon changed.

I had gone to my son's school for a parent-teacher conference. I was walking down the hallway when I saw this award on the bulletin board with my son's name on it. He had submitted an essay and had won an award for it at the state level. I was excited for him at first, not knowing, of course, what the essay was about. Then I read it. It was about why his mother was his hero. In the essay, he talked about the struggles that I thought I had hidden from him, including leaving our house, living in one room, my going to school and helping them study, how I went to work and took care of them, how I always made sure that they were okay and finally, how proud he was of me. I was instantly embarrassed because here was this essay on the wall of a school. Everybody had seen it and everybody now knew that we lived in one room. I thought I had ripped my family apart and here was my son seeing strength when I thought I was a failure in their eyes. All I saw was struggle and shame, but he didn't see it that way. I didn't want my son to feel bad about this, so I simply congratulated him on his award and thanked him for loving me.

We would live like this for six to eight months before I was able to rent a house, and I still didn't tell anyone in my family. I isolated myself and my children for months. I didn't even tell my grandmother what was happening or where we lived. In fact, when my children's father *did* want to see them, I'd have him meet us somewhere. I didn't want anyone to know. I felt like I had to bear that burden alone.

"You can put on a mask, but that doesn't change who you are underneath" (Unknown). I always made sure that no matter what we had, no matter where it came from, that our clothes were cleaned and starched, so our external appearances did not change. The only difference was that now we were dressed up with no home. But I knew how to put on the appearance of being *fine* externally while suffering internally. I had been doing it all of my life.

I was able to find another full-time job in Chesapeake, eventually. At first, we were going to move there, but then my son was accepted into the Governor's School and I didn't want to remove him from this free education and great resources. So I made the choice to drive back and forth between Petersburg and Chesapeake. What should have been an increase became a struggle as I drove two hours in both directions to and from work.

I drove a suburban at the time and gas prices were starting to rise, especially my first summer on the job. I literally slept in my truck some nights because I just could not afford to drive back home. I was spending like $4.99 per gallon in a 44-gallon tank to get to work and home. There were some nights when I had to sleep in my office. I would call home and tell the kids to lock the doors and to not let anyone in. So here I was in a directorship position for a pre-college preparatory program, which had been defunded and I was now bringing it back to success, yet I could not afford to go home. Everything I made went toward gas and trying to keep a roof over our heads. I was successful in my career, but using every dime I had to pay the bills. And there was no child support coming in to alleviate some of the financial stress.

Dr. Nikita C. Garris-Watson

I hated leaving my kids alone and having to have them take care of themselves on those nights. In the beginning, I didn't want them to come on the road with me, but as the summer progressed, I just could not leave them alone anymore. I started to bring them to work with me when I knew I could make it home that night (i.e., put gas in the car). It was just all too much at one time. Something had to give. And it did.

Dr. Nikita C. Garris-Watson

The Last Time

"In my distress I called on the LORD, and cried to my God: he heard my voice out of his temple, and my cry came before him, even into his ears" (Psalm 18:6).

It would be the fourth and final time I would try to take my life. With the failure of my first marriage, the personal destruction of my character, the many health issues that were plaguing me, the loss of my home and the struggle of financial burdens, I fought daily with the spirit of depression. I began to feel that my kids would have been better off without me in their life (at least they would have money, I thought), so driving home from work one night, my intent was to literally have a head on collision. I was a preacher at the time, but it didn't mean that I felt any better about myself. I felt like a failure.

I was driving down Route 460, which is a narrow, two-lane road in each direction. My goal was to run head on into the first truck I saw coming down the opposite road. I was going to swerve out of my lane and let the police say that I was "sleepy." I had it all plotted out. My will was written: my letters to my kids safely tucked away so they would know how much I loved them. If I did manage to survive, I would refuse treatment and just die slowly. I was ready to die, and this time, I would not fail.

I knew the road that I traveled very well; I knew the curve in the road where I would let go of the wheel, the place where I could find the right truck to run into so that I would die instantly. I attempted it more than once that night, but I just couldn't do it. I kept jerking back over into my lane. I didn't want to hit another car or even a semi-truck because I didn't want to kill another family. That's how deeply I plotted to take my life.

Then I saw it: the semi-truck. I had it all planned out how I was going to hit it. Again, I knew exactly when to swerve because of the upcoming curve in the road we were about to take. I knew that if I hit that truck, it would kill me. Death was my plan and right as I reached to prepare myself, I accidently hit the radio button and the song, "I Trust You, Lord," blasted through the suburban. I felt guilt begin to rise up in my spirit instantly. What if I killed the driver? I never wanted to hurt anyone. I also began to wonder about who would take care of my children. My son was now a 9th grader and my daughter was in the 6th grade. Who would love my kids the way I did? I really wanted to see them grow up. How will my children feel? Was I going to leave them broken just like me? Finally, where was my trust? I had said often that I would trust God. Now that trust was being tested.

On that dark, lonely road, I fought a long standing internal battle waging war for my breakthrough. For my entire life, I had struggled against the spirits of suicide and depression with great intensity. The decision had to finally be made that suicide was no longer an option, and it was made that night on the road. Everything didn't get better instantly, however. Let me be clear in saying this. I would see many more struggles and cry many more tears. The difference between that moment and the others before it was that my *mind* had changed. Romans 12:2 says, "Be ye transformed by the renewal of your mind." Therefore, the decision to change my mindset became a personal challenge and responsibility that fateful night. Death could no longer be an option for me when things became unbearable.

I would cry for a long as I drove home that night. I would even ask God what I had done for so much to have happened to me. I would admit to being angry with Him even as I proclaimed my love for Him. That night, part of me did die, but it was the part that had been holding me hostage from freely opening myself up for deliverance within the deeper realms of myself. The decision to live that night opened up a new chapter for me and my destiny.

Chapter 7 ~ Why Me?

"Sometimes the wrong choices bring us to the right places" (Unknown).

Victim of Other People's Choices

My life began with being the innocent bystander of a cycle of poor choices and decisions made by the one person I loved more than anything: my mother's choice to have sex and have me as a teenager, she herself being a victim of her mother's early death and her father's subsequent bad choices, including alcoholism, which I am sure was the result of his own personal struggles and demons. I would struggle severely as the consequence of other people's choices, but then even my choices later in life would cause someone else to suffer consequences. This is what happens when people make bad decisions regardless of the reasons; even in ignorance, there are still consequences that we must live with.

There were moments in my life when the choices and decisions I had to make were predicated by things forced upon me or outside of my control. Equally so, there were consequences that I endured as a result of my own judgments, but it is the realization of my personal choices that have prevented me from playing the victim. I refuse to play the blame game anymore. When situations and circumstances arise, I try to quickly recognize where I fall short, and when dealing with others, I make every effort to understand the motives behind people's decisions and behaviors. My mother's decision to date multiple abusive people was a result of her unresolved childhood traumas and low self-esteem, so her choices became our abuse. I would be a witness to her abuse. I would witness her bad choices, her bad decisions, and this would evoke inside of me feelings that I didn't even want. It is hard to love somebody and yet hate everything about them.

Make no mistake about it, I fiercely love my mother, but I hated everything that she took us through and what she allowed to happen to herself. Watching her year after year, I felt hopeless. You can't, as a child, make an adult's decision for them. You want to, though. You hope that your brokenness will be the reason that they make better choices, but it seemed like as the years went by, she was sinking deeper and deeper into a dark pit that she would never be able to lift herself out of.

I understand all of this differently as an adult now, including what depression and low self-esteem does to a person: how it disconnects you. You can't save somebody when you can't even save yourself. I didn't understand or even know this back then as a child. I didn't understand how someone so beautiful could be so broken. I remember that I would look at her and see her beauty: wrapped in exquisite light-skin with hazel-green eyes, lovely thick, dark, reddish brown hair and tiny waist that complemented her frame perfectly. I just couldn't understand how she could not see that she was beautiful. Why she couldn't see that she was worth more? To watch that beauty become marked by bruises made me sick. I don't think people really think about that what you go through, you take your children through it with you, too.

There were many times that I would jump into the middle of the fights between my mother and whatever boyfriend she was dating at the time or the man she would come to marry to try and protect her. She would get angry with me for trying, and all I wanted to do was to help her. When she hurt, I hurt, and even with the rejection and the abuse, it didn't stop me from loving her. How do you want somebody who doesn't want you? How do you want the love of somebody when everything they say or seems to do is intended to get rid of you?

I did have the 'why me' mentality for many years. Why couldn't I have a father that I could go to? Why did I have to be the one to be molested? Why did I have to be the one to carry the family shame? Why did I have to be the one to be sent away? But I would later come to learn that rejection has the power to be God's protection and direction. I believe that had I stayed in that environment any longer – if I had not been removed and gone to live with my aunts and then my grandmother – I would have eventually succeeded in suicide or simply lost my mind. Being removed from my mother's home, whether I liked how it happened or not, changed the course of my life.

I also still do not know who my father was; I had yet to comprehend why it was that Jeff, the man my mother said was my father, chose not to alleviate the stress of knowing yes or no by taking a blood test and getting it over with. If he was so certain that he was not my father – and he still says he is certain – then why not take the blood test to cancel all doubts and close all mouths? Again, here I am the victim of somebody else's choice. Instead of giving me closure, this person would rather just say, "You're not mine," without physical proof.

But I hold my mother to this same standard. In other words, I am convinced that she is not sure who my father is because with all of my other siblings, she used or pursued child support; with me, she never pursued child support, which says to me that she didn't know because the courts could have settled the matter. So I was now the victim of her indecision or lack of willingness to make a decision as to confirming my paternity.

Finally, in my first marriage, I was a victim of my then husband's decisions to cheat and to bring home to me an STD and then try to use other methods to hide it instead of just telling the truth about what he had done. He could have just come home and admitted to messing up. Now, it would not have been the greatest homecoming, but instead, he chose to put me and our unborn son at the time at risk as I talked about earlier in my story. The irony, however, is that he, too, would bear the burden of my choice not to leave him when the first situation happened. I should have walked away, but I stayed and that decision would result in years of back and forth damage that we would both inflict on one another, and in some ways, even on our children.

All of this created in me a need for closure. I am a person that has to have closure: good bad or indifferent. I have made choices to end or walk away from situations just to get closure even when God may not have been finished with any of it. I have confronted things head on where I am sure that the outcomes could have been better had I spent more time talking it over with God in prayer. Likewise, I have rushed to erroneous conclusions for the sake of closure and spent time in regret that could have been easily avoided had I been patient.

What I would come to realize through all of this is that deliverance is a decision; I had to decide that I wanted better before I could see better in my life. However, wanting was not enough; it also required the work of dealing with the hidden issues of my mind and heart. Facing me was a strenuous part of the journey because there was no hiding from myself and doing so demanded that I do it daily. For years, looking in the mirror was the hardest thing I faced day-to-day as no amount of makeup could hide what I saw looking back at me. I wrestled with finding peace with the pieces of my life that needed to be pulled together; however, unlike a puzzle, I would have to work the middle before putting together the edges. Change would come sometimes swiftly and other times, excruciatingly slow; yet each step, no matter how small, was a step of victory.

Chapter 8 ~ Protection vs. Overprotective

"Real protection means teaching your children to manage risks on their own. Not shielding them from every hazard" (Wendy Mogel).

Living in a Silo: The Girl with No Last Name

I am a Garris, but my siblings have different last names, and they can attach those names to a person. I cannot; Garris is my mother's maiden name, and so I can only attach it to her, leaving me with little to no legacy to go with it. There was nothing good about that name that I could see when I was growing up because no one around me with that name was accomplishing anything positive with their life. We were poor, lived in the hood, my grandfather (mother's father) was a drunk and my uncle had molested me. My mother was in and out of abusive relationships and having children with different fathers and last names. As a young girl, I could not see what was good about the Garris name. My one uncle who shared my last name and was doing well in comparison was in the military and so far away that I knew very little about his accomplishments, so it would be much later in life before I would see any sort of positive spin on the legacy.

For me, it was like I was not only carrying a tainted life, but a tainted name. I was having an identity crisis not knowing who my father was so that I could carry his last name. As if to provoke my pain, it seemed like everyone around me had their father's name, but not me. I didn't know to whom I belonged or even where I belonged. Bearing the burden of this shame and uncertainly, as I grew up and even when I became a parent, I began to live my life compartmentalized. Different "aunts, uncles and cousins" had been accumulated and collected throughout the years, but none of them really "belonged" to me. They were special people, but still not my "family." I didn't want to explain to the people I was dating or to my children who all of these people were because we all had different names or unexplainable connections. It was too much.

For a long time, I did not let people get close to me or my children. I didn't let them get to know my personal business. I kept my life separate: my personal life, professional life and spiritual life. Everything was kept in these little boxes, and as much as possible, I tried to not let those worlds connect, but God did not create us to be alone. He strategically placed people in my life who were able to get past my walls of defense. I am still protective of myself – of who I am, part of it stemming from not knowing how to deal with people. I admit that I had a social handicap, so to speak; that is the by-product of having spent most of my life trying to hide secrets or because I simply didn't have answers to my own questions. I found myself operating from a perpetual place of disconnect or distrust.

When you live in a silo, you create these walls that you use in an attempt to protect yourself from being hurt or even hurting other people. You operate by yourself, and that is what I did for most of my life. I spent a lot of time by myself, and I had to ask myself if that was a good thing or a damaging thing. Because of the dysfunction in my family, including not knowing who my father was, trying to handle what had happened in my mother's household, and being oblivious as to how to explain to my kids who the different people were coupled with the confusion that I was carrying, I kept them away from everybody. I considered it my way of protecting them from the brokenness of our family.

Even today, I am not sure if that was the best thing to do, but I did not want to have to explain why there were so many different last names, so many titles with unexplainable family attachments. I did not want to defend why this person was called 'auntie' or that person was called 'uncle,' and then try and clarify why this person was not their "real" grandparent and so much more. To me, it was all so problematic that I believed by keeping everyone on the parameters, I was protecting them. My greatest fear was that they would be rejected or hurt and I had made up my mind that as long as it was in my power to protect them, I would do so at any cost. I never wanted them to feel how I did: to love someone and then feel so lonely when that love was not returned. I knew too well the pain of wanting to find my place in the midst of a gathering and despite how kind everyone was to me, to still feel alone in a group of people.

They do know my foster grandmother very well, however; she was the first person I took them to see when they were born, but I never really discussed with them who she *really* is. I also never felt a need to protect them from her; I had watched her embrace too many "unwanted" people and make them feel like family. I knew that if I could trust anyone to treat them with love, I could trust her. I would watch with tear-filled eyes as she would welcome them into the world and family with the same enthusiasm that she did her biological grandchildren. Once again, she did not let me down. She has been a consistent presence in both my life and theirs.

I didn't really think about what I was doing or how my choices might have a negative effect on my children until we went to a family function to celebrate my grandmother and people were asking them if they knew who they were. My children responded with hesitant no's looking at me inquisitively with the desire to not be rude, but having to be honest. I realized then just how much I had kept them away from different environments and people. These people were really good people that they would have enjoyed knowing, but I did not want the task or burden of having to make it all make sense. In a sense, I was being protective, but in hindsight, I was being overprotective. My children did not get to know some wonderful people, and that is heartbreaking because I have some people in my grandmother's family, for example, my godmother and aunts, whom they really do not know at all. They know their father's immediate siblings and their families, but they really do not know extended family on either side.

In spite of myself, I would come to understand the love of God and His infinite wisdom for knowing what we need even when we don't know that we need it. As the kids and I were going through a tough season in life right after the separation and pending divorce, while I was sick and as we faced our homelessness, there was a family in the church – the White family – that adopted us. God was so gracious to us. A large and loving family, without a clear reason, seemingly, all at the once, the entire family embraced us as members. Having no idea what we were facing, they invited us to every family gathering not accepting no for an answer. For over two years, they would hold us close going so far as to celebrate all of our birthdays the first year. The matriarch of the family, clearly guided by God, would call at the most unexpected moments to speak life. The siblings and their spouses would claim my children and call them their own not allowing them to miss one opportunity. This family was not rich by society's standards, but they were wealthy in love and deposited it into the three of us freely.

I remember one day when my son said he wished he had that much family, and I realized just how much my children did not have. So, I was so appreciative for this family that literally stepped in and made us feel loved, welcomed. They were like a pseudo-family for us.

I will forever be indebted to the White family for the part they played in that season of our lives. They gave my children aunts, uncles and cousins that they really did not have. While one portion of our family dynamic was breaking up, again, God was so gracious to give us a pseudo/substitute family to take their place.

This is even more so what I mean about living in a silo. My decisions were not inherently bad as it is the responsibility of every parent to protect their children as best they can. It was my methods and motives that needed to be altered. If parents are not careful, our fears can become our children's fears inadvertently. It took time for me to learn how to love my children and still let go. For instance, God would present a great dilemma to me one evening as I was driving. He asked me, "Who do you love more? Me or your children?" I would immediately feel dread hit my chest as I felt that I was being asked to choose between my God who had saved me and my children that I loved with everything in me.

I drove for 45 minutes weeping and trying to understand the purpose behind God's question. I thought back to how Abraham must have felt when God asked him about Isaac. I tossed and turned internally and then with hesitation replied, "God, I love you more, but I certainly love my children." In the tender way in which only God can do, he replied back, "Then trust me to protect them because I love them more than you do."

God was freeing me from fears that I didn't realize had a hold on me. He wasn't trying to keep me from loving and protecting my children. He was showing me that loving them included entrusting them to Him. My prayers for my children would change that day and my practices would follow. What I did know was that God would be with them when I was with them and when I was not. I knew that God understood my heart's cry to give them what I had been not able to, not materially, but mentally. I was beginning to understand better the heart of God as a Father who sent a Savior.

Admittedly, I did and still do have trust issues. I am still cautious, but because of my role as a pastor and leader, I am more engaged in different aspects of peoples' lives. I find that I have to lean more heavily on God to guide my interactions with those He has placed in my care or that I am divinely connected to because that area of my life is still protected to a degree. There was a time where I did not mix the personal, professional and spiritual aspects of my life. I had them in different compartments where they functioned independently. They've all become so intertwined now. At moments I look around in awe when I see that the ministry in all of its diversity has become my family. I am still ferociously protective of those that I love; this is the nature of who I was created to be. Some days, it is a struggle for me to be who God created me to be versus what life tried to shape me into becoming. It's like going through a continuous metamorphosis, and I am so grateful because I am walking in my destiny.

Chapter 9 ~ Beauty for Ashes

"3 To appoint unto them that mourn in Zion, to give unto them beauty for ashes, the oil of joy for mourning, the garment of praise for the spirit of heaviness; that they might be called trees of righteousness, the planting of the Lord, that he might be glorified" (Isaiah 61:3).

The Power of Forgiveness

When something ugly happens to you, it takes time to forge forward and, ultimately, to forgive. I had so much that I needed to let go of; the anger wasn't helping me or taking me anywhere, the bitterness still had me broken, the hurt was a hindrance and the pain was a problem. Everything had me bound spiritually, emotionally and psychologically, and I was dealing with the consequences physically as well. Before God could allow me to be of any use, I had to be ministered to repeatedly in all of these areas. I had to take the broken places to God. I had to go and cry. I had to tell God that I was angry with Him, and, of course, to most people, that's the greatest sin in the world. But I needed to be free enough to tell Him that I was angry with Him. That I was disappointed. I felt left down.

Admittedly, I tried to hide from God for a long time before that like He couldn't see me or hear my thoughts. For me, I thought that if I did not say these things, then it didn't give it any validity. But then I got to a place where I had to say it. I had to receive God's response; I had to receive both His correction and His protection, and in the midst of all of that, receive His love. My anger and disappointment were my truths, and the word tells us that they that worship Him must worship Him in spirit and in truth (John 4:24). God already knew what I was thinking and what I was feeling was that getting past this truth would open me up to worship God freely. So I had to deal with me first – the broken places – in order to get beauty for ashes. I had to take Him the ashes of my life; I had to be willing to expose myself.

Exposure required me to also acknowledge where I had disappointed Him. When God shows you yourself in entirety, it's easy to point fingers at others, but it's not easy to sort out the role we play in our own lives. Again, I don't believe in the abuse excuse, and so while I may not have thought about it when I was raising my children, I still was negligent in some other things. I didn't do everything I needed to do as a believer and I am convinced my pain at some points prevented me from being a better parent, so I had to deal with my shortcomings, my failures: my everything.

Forgiveness was not a process that happened over night. I think about the movie, *Shrek*, where the donkey told Shrek he was like an onion; he had to peel back the layers to get to the real Shrek. This process of forgiveness and healing was like peeling back the layers of my life. And I had to start with the first act of molestation and everything that was subsequent to that moment.

The first person I had to forgive was myself. I had to forgive myself for my mistakes, for my promiscuity, for being angry and for what I felt like were my failures. The process to forgiveness started with me for me. I was very critical of myself; I could see everything I had done wrong. God allowed me to understand that if nothing else, I had survived. He began to show me the ministry of my mistakes – the possibilities of my problems. All of this became a part of my process, but, again, when you peel something, it's still a tearing away. There were and are still painful moments. Similarly, I had to learn to genuinely be vulnerable before God. I would go to places alone like conferences where people did not know me or know my name. People would often look at me and make assumptions about who and what I was. That was very difficult for me. But I just wanted to be alone with God in these places. He had a work to do in me. I would experience private deliverance in public places searching for what I could not obtain in my private times with God. It should be noted that while there is power to be found in private, intimate moments with God, the word tells us with significant reason to, "forsake not the assembling of ourselves" as God has a way of using the collective gathering of His people to ensure that everyone makes great spiritual gains (Hebrews 10:25).

Then I had to begin to forgive people, which is still a daily process because I had to forgive people for an apology I would never actually receive. If I had waited on that apology, I'd still be stuck to this day. Forgiveness is more for self than for others because the word of God tells us to forgive so that we might be forgiven (Matthew 6:14). So countless times, I forgave because I could not afford to not to be forgiven by God. I knew that I had done stuff or would do stuff that would warrant me needing to be forgiven, so my first level of forgiveness was that I wanted to be forgiven. And then I got into the deeper parts of forgiveness.

The most freeing thing that I came to realize was that forgiveness did not necessarily mean reconciliation. That I was not required to necessarily try and maintain interaction with the offending party if it was not healthy. That I could respectfully have boundaries; it wasn't giving the person a "Free Pass." That is for God to handle. It allowed me, however, to move past it mentally and emotionally. It wasn't saying that what they did or said to me was okay, or that I agreed with it; it was saying that it happened, but I refuse to get stuck right here. I lived my life "stuck" for a long time and because I had not forgiven; it began to fuel other decisions for which I paid the consequences, including staying in the wrong marriage for too long, trying to get even when I could have walked away, seeking to make others suffer the way they had made me suffer and living with burning bitterness. It was toxic and I was drinking the poison while waiting for others to die.

The first time I experienced true forgiveness, the freedom that came with it fueled my continued pursuit. Sometimes you can be bound so badly that you don't even realize you are bound until you are set free. I found that to be my story. I did not realize how many things were holding me hostage until that moment. It was like I could breathe again.

Let's look at it from another perspective or illustration: the baby elephant who is born with a rope tied to its leg. When it is a baby, the rope is there to contain it, but because it has spent its whole life with that rope tied around its leg, even when it becomes an adult and has the physical strength to break that rope, it won't because it does not realize it has that kind of strength. I was glad to realize that I had the ability to break the ropes tied on me early in life. I had the strength. I could have easily stayed in a place where I said, "This happened to me and that happened to me," but I began to understand that the longer I was held hostage to those things, it was as if it was still happening to me. But the moment I was able to say I forgive or the moment I was able to be done with it and walk away, it wasn't happening to me anymore. The moment I was able to say I forgive or the moment I was able to be done with it and walk away, I took control.

Forgiveness gave me back control over my life. It gave me the control that I had never had before, and I refuse, after spending so much of my life where others' choices made decisions for me, to be controlled by others' choices anymore. That is not to say that things still do not hurt me because they do. Do things still bother me? Yes. Like many people, I have been betrayed and mistreated, but I refuse to stay there. Sometimes it's a daily process of forgiveness therapy; and sometimes it's hourly because there are some things that just tick me off. I am human. But I purpose myself when certain feelings and emotions come up to give them over to God. Unaddressed anger is ammunition for the enemy.

A recent talk with God allowed me to understand that certain things later in my life where permitted to happen in order to teach me how to recover quickly. I recognize that by the grace and mercy of God that I do, in fact, have the ability to recover quickly, to heal more rapidly than what even I expected. I think about the character Wolverine from the movie *X-Men*. He had the ability even after being wounded to self-heal. I feel like a spiritual wolverine in that I can receive wounds, but it's the power of God in me that leads me to His presence where I heal. God's presence is the healing balm that allows me to recover.

I want to make sure that the altar of my heart is pure because the word in Psalm 24:4 tells us that only clean hands and a pure heart will be able to enter into God's presence. I want to know that I have access to God's presence, and I don't want what someone else has done to me to deny me of that access.

Part II

Now What!

Chapter 10 ~ The Ministry of Transparency

"2 The only letter of recommendation we need is you yourselves. Your lives are a letter written in our hearts; everyone can read it and recognize our good work among you. 3 Clearly, you are a letter from Christ showing the result of our ministry among you. This "letter" is written not with pen and ink, but with the Spirit of the living God. It is carved not on tablets of stone, but on human hearts" (2 Corinthians 3:2-3).

My ministry is that of deliverance and transparency, and in it, I see a lot of brokenness. Because of this, I no longer have the perspective of "Why me?" I grew to accept it as the journey of my life. While I don't believe that it was God's perfect will, it happened. I have accepted that God saved me to sacrifice me as a servant for the Kingdom allowing me the privilege to appreciate that God has a way to make all things work together for our good (Romans 8:28).

I two read books by T.D. Jakes called *Can You Stand to Be Blessed*? and *Why? Because You're Anointed*. These two books were prevalent in my deliverance. When we begin to look at the things in our life differently, it changes our perspective. People talk about the paradigm shift; well, that is what I experienced moment by moment as I struggled to find my way during my spiritual pilgrimage. It would take years through a long process to find my healing; however, with each experience, I was able to look at my life differently. I had new eyesight, which gave me new insight!

The reality was that I did not die; I wasn't defeated. I had fallen, but I had not failed. I should have been dead or somewhere crazy. I should have succumbed to so many things, but I have come to understand the scripture in Psalm 34:18 where it says God is close to the broken-hearted and saves those who are crushed in spirit. I have come to understand first-hand what it says in Proverbs 18:10 that the name of the Lord is a strong tower; the righteous who run to it are safe. Calling on His name, and although I do not always feel Him, knowing that He is there. Now this all took time; it was not something that happened over night.

Being transparent enough to talk about my life took time. I had to take it moment by moment, hour by hour, to get from the *Why Me?* to the *Why Not Me?* Do I still at times wish my life had been different? Yes. Nobody wants the burden of what I went through. Nobody seeks to carry the shame of the story. I cannot change the past, but I can change my mindset. The first time that I was allowed to sit down with someone who was broken in the same places I had been, to hold their hand and pray them through it, changed me. Where I was once a victim, I now wanted to help other people find victory. I knew there was no turning back.

I had a hard conversation with God one day; it was a major moment of clarity for me. I was sitting on the side of my bed; it was the end of my first marriage and the night before I was scheduled to have surgery to determine if I had breast cancer. I cried out, "God, I want to change my life!" I was talking about the impending divorce, the pain in the marriage, my health issues and the hurt of my past.

"What are you willing to give up?" He asked. I heard Him so clear in my spirit asking me this question that I responded back immediately.

"I want to give up the pain, the brokenness. I want to give up the hurt."

He said, "But if you give up these pieces of your life, what else are you willing to sacrifice?" I didn't understand what God was asking until He said, "Are you willing to give up what you've accomplished? Are you willing to give up your children? Are you willing to give up what you learned? The strength you have gained?"

It was in that moment that I understood. My story was the ability to turn struggle into strength; my fight came from my failures. And so to give up the bad would have made me a different person. I wouldn't have the fortitude that I had developed. Those who believe in God often talk about faith as if it is a fairytale of wishing and waiting. Faith is NOT the absence of fear; it is having everything in the world to be afraid of and *still* doing it. That's the faith I had cultivated through the chaos. Usually, it is when it doesn't make sense that your faith must respond with action.

Now I can't say that I've never had doubt: I have. In fact, I still have moments of *great* doubt. But there comes a time and place where destiny demands that you deliver. My destiny was greater than my damage. I have also learned that I do not do well with the unknown. Those seasons that we go through with God where we don't know what's happening or which way He is taking us, those are typically, my most agonizing seasons. However, my relationship with God has taught me to trust the process and the God who made the promise.

I now understand that only God can take such an ugly set of circumstances and use them with such efficacy that I can embrace the words found in Isaiah 61:3, "He gives you beauty for ashes, oil of joy for mourning, the garment of praise for heaviness," and know what that truly means. He is, in spite of everything, creating a masterpiece because He is the Master. It didn't and doesn't always look or feel good, and I don't always like every part of the process of creating a masterpiece, but what I decided is that if my brokenness can help somebody else – if I could save somebody else from going through what I went through for so long – if I could speak like where there is death – if I could take my pain and turn it into power – then that is what I would do. I would fight with my life.

For some people, certain scriptures become life for them. One such lifeline for me is Jeremiah 29:11-14a (NLT): "11 For I know the plans I have for you," says the Lord. "They are plans for good and not for disaster, to give you a future and a hope. 12 In those days when you pray, I will listen. 13 If you look for me wholeheartedly, you will find me. 14 I will be found by you," says the Lord." I didn't know what to expect when I was going *through*, but God did, and as I sought Him, He was faithful to be found.

Chapter 11 ~ Sometimes, I feel like a Motherless Child

Mommy, Dearest

My vision of my mother would evolve over the years. While I have and always will love her, other feelings would take precedence. There was a season where my prevalent perspective of my mother was hate. I hated what she allowed. I hated that I felt like she had never protected me, and I hated that she did not protect herself. Up until my late 20s, I lived my life striving not to be anything like her. Everything that I associated with the negativity of a female, I attributed to her. So I didn't want a man who felt like he could control me; I didn't want children because I felt like what I had seen growing up would make me a bad mother. I hated what I felt was her decision to choose other people over me every time.

I knew that I did not want to struggle, so getting to school, being there and not failing was everything. If I failed, then I was like my mother, and I could not have that. Failing was not an option for me. I never felt smart enough, but my nightmares haunted me too much to give in. I believed that if I did fail, I'd end up back at her house or end up with multiple children by different men, so I had to become *something*. At one point in my life, I wanted to be a lawyer to defend abused and neglected children because I felt like they needed a voice. Then I realized that the field was too personal for me to be objective. I knew I would not be able to separate fact from fiction without a sense of compromised judgement. I was able to *see* that it was not a good decision for me.

Dr. Nikita C. Garris-Watson

I felt like my mother had made poor decisions as I was growing up. I remember when she married Stanley and after they had been married three years, she decided to have an actual wedding. I actually said to her, "We're poor. Why are you trying to have a wedding?" Now that was out of order for a child to say, but it was true. I was always a realist or a good observer. If we're struggling, what sense does it make to have a wedding? These truths that came from me as a child infuriated her.

I remember when she got pregnant with my youngest brother; she took me on a drive to tell me she was pregnant. This was only a few months before I was removed from her home. When she told me, I said, "But we're already struggling with four of us, why would you punish a fifth person?"

It never appeared that she was ever trying to get out of what we were in; it was as if she were comfortable in confusion and calamity. That she had decided this was going to be her life. I was frustrated by her because I could see that she could do and be more. If she were to just get away from "these no-good people," maybe she could *see* it. I hated it. I wanted my siblings out of these horrific situations.

I hated that she would not believe me about what had happened to me at the hands of her brother or her husband. I had not even bothered to tell her the others horrors that I had endured at the hands of other family members. Out of everyone that *did* believe me, to have the one person at that point that mattered the most to me not believe me was probably *the* most devastating. To want her to be proud of me, to celebrate my accomplishments, I have always wanted that, but I never got it.

But as I began to heal from my own stuff, my perspective about my mother began to change. As God began to allow me to understand her story, my emotions progressed from hate to that of painful pity. I pitied her.

I felt sorry that she couldn't see who she really could have been. I felt sorry that she couldn't be motivated to come out of her own situation. I literally wanted to shake her, to wake her up because it seemed like she was trapped in this place of unconsciousness. She was like the walking dead, almost. And so I realized that my mother must have felt that she was stuck – that she was in a place where she needed a Damascus Road experience with God to get better.

Still, I also felt like she could get better if she *tried*. She was always self-sacrificing because she was trying to be loved, but by the wrong people. God began to show me that she had her own demons that she was fighting with; out of her five siblings, she is the youngest and the only one that is light-skinned. It made her stand out – not fit in. Out of all of them, she looks the most like their mother and even carries her name, but she was denied the right to really get to know her mother because she was robbed of that opportunity by her untimely death. To make matters worse, her family had not allowed her to go to the funeral. She, essentially, did not get to say goodbye to her mother. My mother never got the chance to grieve the loss of her mother.

In the rare moments where she would share stories of her childhood after the death of her mother, it was clear that her choices were always around trying to be loved. The truth is, I don't know that my mother ever saw her own strength. I would watch her start many projects with great enthusiasm and then fall short of finishing them to the end. For example, she'd start school, and then drop out. She'd start writing a book (she has the gift of writing), but would never see it all the way through. I think her fear of failure was so strong that it prevented her from seeing anything through to finality. I would watch with frustration feeling deep within myself that if she could see that *one* thing through, it would break the cycle in her life. I would read her many written works that the world should be privileged to share and shake my head knowing that they were being denied access to some of God's most prolific expressions on paper. I would see the potential that she possessed and sit by helplessly (even now as an adult) not knowing what it was going to take to have the scales removed from her eyes.

I remember being angry with her when my youngest sister got pregnant. I went to the house one day to see my precious new nephew and my mother had the bassinet in her room. I became instantly frustrated because I knew that she was now going to take on the role of "mother" when that was my sister's job. And she did. My sister never dealt with those consequences; now here we are six kids later, and my mother is raising five of them (one child is deceased). She is trying to save someone else and not herself. This is where I think she got her sense of worth from: in trying to save other people. Save everyone that is except for me.

After thinking hard on this, however, I've come to realize that my mother didn't think I needed saving. Once I was removed from her home, I think she got to a place within herself where she felt like I could take care or save myself. What she didn't understand or know was that my strength had to come; it was not already there within me.

I still, in some ways, feel sorry for her, but I've now moved into focused and consistent prayers for her. I tried to take her away a few times to help her catch her breath so that she could get her head together, but she would not go by herself. She'd either put it off, make excuses or she always wanted to bring someone with her, never fully understanding that I wanted her to have just a few moments alone for herself.

In 2014, my mother sent me a letter. At the time, she and Stanley were members of our church, but they had stopped coming and had limited interactions. This behavior was not uncommon in the time that they had been with us, so I assumed that perhaps health issues, personal issues or the demands of raising five young children had taken their toll. I was not aware of anything that had been said or done to precipitate their disappearance. Now one may ask how I handled the situation having to lead those who had hurt me, and my answer is God. Forgiveness and healing will allow you to do what you never thought possible. I was extremely cautious in never allowing our past to be known to anyone in the church and I made every effort to treat them with love.

When I saw the letter, my instincts were immediately on alert. In it, she stated that my testimony about the things that had happened to me in the past were getting to her; people were "talking" and asking her questions, which I found difficult to understand because I rarely discussed my past with the congregation or even publicly. Even in sharing what I did, I never gave enough details to damage the life of anyone. Understanding that people would, of course, know who my mother was without her being named, I was always very protective of her and was careful about what I said. Still, I'd share what was necessary to help in places where people were broken. My ministry was not built on my brokenness, but on God's goodness and I included my testimony only as led.

I read the letter with a sense of disbelief and awe. She was accusing me of trying to build a platform off my story of abuse. For 10 handwritten pages, I read words that pierced me, ripping off old scar tissue and inflicting new wounds. God had to work with me in that moment and show me what the truth was about the letter. I am never one who wants to be seen or be in the limelight in that way. He had to counteract what was being said and done in that letter. He said, "The enemy always has a way of pointing you in the direction I am trying to take you."

Paradoxically, two days prior, the Lord had been on me about writing this book and I had been weeping. He was asking me do something again that was going to ostracize or isolate me because many of the people in this book are still alive and present. I had been incessantly fighting Him about telling my story. I had wrestled with God for eight years about not wanting my life to be available for misuse or to be thought of as a story to destroy the lives of others. So, when the letter arrived, it was to show me that whether I wrote the book or not, there would always be warfare about my life. God had a plan to heal people through my story and I was in a tug of war with Him about going "public." I would hear Isaiah 61:7 over and over in my spirit: "For your shame ye shall have double; and for confusion [you] shall rejoice in [your] portion..." I was never going to be able to appease people and please God at the same time, so "Do what I told you to do," He said.

Did I want to appease man or God? Did I want to make God angry or man? I proceeded to call my sister to make sure that I wasn't in my flesh. I strongly believe that everyone should have in their life accountability persons, especially those who are "anointed" or are in positions of power that spend time with God; you have to have someone in your life who doesn't mind checking you not for criticism, but for construction. My sister is one of those checkpoints for me. Though I don't like to draw people into situations, especially those who are close to those involved, I shared some of the letter with her. I asked her what she thought. Her reply was freeing. She said, "Do what God said do."

I think, more than anything, I was offended by what was in the letter. With all that had happened, all the forgiveness that I had tried to extend in both directions to all parties involved, all the praying and fasting I had done for him when he was in the hospital, all the ways I tried help them, and I was still being treated this way. I was genuinely offended, but I knew I could not stay there. Offense opens up the door to too many things, so I had to decide that it was not worth it. But despite my deliverance, this did not happen all at once. I would have to fight the voices in my head every time the words written on the pages replayed themselves. I would have to lay my heart before God as bitterness tried to rise up. I would have to buckle my knees in prayer as old pain and new pain converged in my heart. I would have to silence my spirit as I tossed and turned with the idea of confronting my accusers and abusers in anger. I would have to break my will to want to fight in my own defense. I would have to tame my temper as I tossed away the thoughts that did not line up with the word of God. My spirituality and my humanity would fight daily, but deliverance would come.

Interestingly, I would not see or talk to my mother for six months after I got the letter. When I did see her eventually at a function my sister was hosting, I would not engage with her and my step-father. I didn't try to pretend that everything was okay; I let them have their space and left. I didn't want to hurt my sister or to make her and her guests feel uncomfortable. So here it was again that I was trying to make others feel good and took on that burden, and because of that, I was not able to spend time with my family. But at least the situation was now in my control. I was not being put out.

A year after receiving the letter, my mother showed up at one of our conferences. My sister was preaching as part of it. Surprisingly, she came by herself and I embraced her. My thing was that regardless of what she thought or what the enemy was whispering in her ear, I wanted her to know that I was not her enemy. So I embraced her and went on about doing what I was supposed to do because she was there for my sister, not for me. She later wrote a message on Facebook about the conference and how well my sister had ministered and how much growth she had seen; she ended with the words, "Although my oldest daughter does not believe me, I am so proud of her, too." She did not tag me in the message, but God allowed me to see it in that moment. I sat at my desk that day and simply whispered, "I love you, too," choosing to leave well enough alone.

The Sunday before she moved to another state, she came to the church; interestingly, that morning, I had been praying for her and my youngest sister. To look up and see her walk in was very surprising, but to see her and still not be able to reach her was devastating. Even with all that had happened, I just wanted to take her out of her situation and show her that there's more to life for her. She clearly has this agonizing relationship with God where I believe that she loves Him and, at times, wants better, but does not believe that she can be a recipient of what others have received. Even after crying, and shedding tears, there has to be a movement; there has to be a willingness to change. She will cry to God and say she wants better, but I've never seen her follow through for herself. I have even watched her motivate and encourage others in moments of spiritual strength only to deny that same power to herself. This is why all I can do now is pray for her.

I am not angry. I don't have the necessity to be angry. I watch her life from the sidelines in sympathy wishing I could change her story, but, ultimately, I have come to the place where all I *can* do for her is to pray, and pray her strength. Pray peace for her; pray that she will have peace even for what happened in my life. I've told my mother publically and privately, "You can't change what happened to me. God has used what happened to take me to where I am now."

Many times, my mother would sit in church and weep during my sermons out of guilt, I presume, but it was not necessary because I had forgiven her. I have moved forward in freedom. Now I need for her to forgive herself. What happened to me is no longer my burden; it has become my blessing. Genesis 50: 20 puts it best: "[the enemy] intended to harm me, but God intended it all for good. He brought me to this position so I could save the lives of many people." If God can do that for me, and teach me how to do that for others, allow me to be a living epistle, bring me through years of bad choices made upon being broken, and I am still here? I tell people, I am a whole lot of things, but crazy ain't one of them. That's a God-thing!

There are still countless moments of challenge for my self-esteem. I am not a perfected thing; I am being perfected. The word of God teaches us that we are being taken from glory to glory, becoming more like God as we spend time with Him allowing Him to show us the areas in our lives that still need to be spiritually adjusted. But I am strong enough now to allow the process to take place. There were times in my life when I couldn't go through the process – couldn't endure the process. I hurt for those who can't or won't allow themselves to go through the process, and sometimes that process is just facing ourselves – our inner most thoughts and demons and feelings. I've learned to allow myself to be okay with myself. I like my "me time" – maybe a little too much - ☺ - because I can get in my head, my thoughts.

I want to see my mother make it. I still believe in her. I am still my mother's cheerleader, but if I had stopped to save her, I would have succumbed to sorrow. I've had to learn to love and let others grow at their own pace.

Chapter 12 ~ I Do...Again

"They that sow in tears shall reap in joy" (Psalm 126:5).

Joy for Sorrow

When I think about my second marriage, I call it "Joy for Sorrow" because I call my husband the answer to my prayers wrapped in flesh. He embodies years of what I've asked God for. Maybe not always knowing what I was looking for as I would move in and out of relationships, but when I would cry out about where I was or what I had or didn't have, I didn't realize that I would actually find it in another person.

Psalm 126:5 says, "They that sow in tears shall reap in joy." My current husband is the first person that ever made me feel protected. When he came into my life, we had a real conversation; we were introduced by a mutual acquaintance and we first started talking to one another over the phone. We had talked extensively before we actually met and we were able to talk about the important things.

The first time we spoke over the phone, we talked for eight hours non-stop. He had previously been married for 12 years and I had been married for 14. Having been married before, and that long, you tend to come into the second relationship with a no nonsense approach; for instance, when I was first divorced, I was very protective of who was around my children. As a victim of molestation, you should be protective of who is around your children. Anyone I dated who requested to meet my children, I considered them to be a pedophile, which was probably not a fair judgment, but I preferred to keep them safe now than to be sorry later. That's how I thought about it because in my thinking, meeting my children should not have been anyone's first priority or focus. Meeting the children was something that was earned over time.

In the five years between my first and second marriage, I dated periodically, but having gained the wisdom to lay everything before God for examination, I tried to quickly learn who belonged in my life and who did not; everyone is not a part of your destiny, and that does not make them good or bad. They are just not to be a part of your life. I did, however, come to have three more consistent connections. The first one was a person from my past who had his own unresolved healing process to complete and was quickly removed from my life. The second was a good person, but I mistook why God had allowed our lives to connect. I was there to help him find his way back to God. I was supposed to minister to him, not be in a relationship with him. The third person was the one that would be most shocking to me, a minister himself who told me that I had too much ministry in me. Outwardly, we had many things in common and shared goals and ideas of what we wanted to see happen in the church. Despite my reluctance to consider a relationship, we actually talked about marriage and many other things, but I would later learn he was intimidated by what he saw God doing in me and in my life. So, when he could not get to me to walk away from ministry, he decided to walk away from me. That's when I realized, again, that rejection is God's protection.

It protected me from being in another marriage where I would have been in competition with my husband or in a marriage where I would have been miserable. What was interesting also about the end of this connection was that I mourned for a very short period. You would think that if you were really supposed to be with someone, then the mourning period would be much longer. I remember literally lying on the couch as we were talking on the phone; I felt like I deserved more information as to why he was breaking up with me. When I got off the phone, I processed what had been said and then soon realized that I was better off without him. When you are single, you miss the interaction with other people for a period, but then you realize that this is better for you. There are some things that God will take out of your heart so quickly so that you do not mourn what you should not mourn any longer.

I met James eight months later. The number eight symbolizes new beginnings and I was privileged with a new beginning. At that time in my life, I had a very specific requirement of anyone who wanted to be in my life. They had to read the book, *The Five Love Languages*, and anybody who do not read it or want to, was automatically disqualified. It was my perspective that if you could not take the time to read it, then you weren't *the one*. That book so clearly articulated what was needed, especially for me, as I knew my chapters and my pages.

Having shared wisdom from the pages during our phone conversations, I set out to buy the book for my husband on our first date. Amusingly, when I went to purchase the book, it was on sale – a special edition, leather copy. It looked so manly, so I brought him some roses, the book (I had it gift wrapped) and a card. We met outside of the bookstore and when he got into my car, I had all of it waiting for him lying in his seat. His initial reaction was surprise because he had never received flowers before; he had always given them, but never received. It was good to be a "first" in his life

We got in my car, and I took him to one of my favorite places to pray by a lake that was not too far from where I lived. I figured if anything was going to come out spiritually, it was going to come out by that water.

Dr. Nikita C. Garris-Watson

Or if he was crazy, I was going to drown him. Kidding. ☺ Anyway, we talked about life and so many things; it was the most natural conversation I ever had with someone. He even told me that he had prayed about our meeting that day and was able to tell me things that God had said pertaining to us. The fact that he had taken the time to pray before we had even connected was a moment of awareness for me because it showed me that he understood the nature of who I was and what was important to me: prayer was the pillar of my existence. Hearing from God was important to me.

We sat there that evening and talked for over three hours before we went to dinner. Having asked him during our first conversation what he was looking for, and his answer being stability, we would explore this topic in greater detail as I asked him to define what that meant to him, which he explained. He would turn then the tables and asked me to help him understand my previous answers to him as I had expressed the requirements of consistency and honesty. I explained to him how I would rather face an ugly truth than a pretty lie. I told him that I knew I was not girlfriend material, nor was I willing to compromise in being someone's lover, but that in God's timing, I knew that I was designed to be a wife. His soft chuckle would light up the car as he expressed that he had never heard it put that way before. We talked extensively about what I felt that meant and how I had come to that conclusion. There was an unspoken expectation in those hours of openness that here was no room to present false images of who we wanted to be, but rather to accept who we really were.

We would spend more time together over the next few weeks, and then we decided to go away together for the weekend to discuss if we were going to have a serious relationship or part company and not waste each other's time. Again, when you are at a certain age in your life, you just don't have that time to waste anymore.

While he shared that a man knows what he wants, I made it clear to him that I did not believe in five or 10 year dating relationships. So we decided to go away and have a real heart to heart conversation with the explicit understanding that this was *not* going to be a sexual situation because there was just too much at stake.

We went to a hotel in Virginia Beach where there was no phone or TV. I had asked for 36 hours of his time, but it turned into 48. The first night while at dinner, we talked some more about our wants and needs; the next day, we would agree to meet early for prayer and to continue our conversation. As we sat having a heart-to-heart, he was overcome with emotion and fell to his knees in prayer. Feeling the burden of his pain, I placed his head in my lap and prayed as he wept. I prayed for him the only way that I knew how: with urgency and fervency trying to reach God. Everything he had been facing for years alone had hit him all at once; and I prayed for him until he found his strength. We hung out together for the rest of the day just talking and being present, and the rest is history, as they say. We would come to call that weekend U.D.A. (undivided attention). It means that we do not want to share the other party with the world; it is our time alone together. No children, no family, no ministry; it's our time.

In the beginning of our relationship, he was a truck driver and he had asked me if I could handle being married to someone who drove a truck. Initially, I said yes, but less than a year into our relationship, I hated it with everything in me. ☺ He never gave me a reason to distrust him, which to me was a release after having been in a marriage where you couldn't trust anything or anyone. The thing is that, at this point, I had learned to put my trust in God, not man, and allow Him to protect me even from me.

I would see my husband evolve day by day as time went on. I would learn about his past and his pain, his potential and his promise all at the same time. I would see his gift, his calling that had only been marginally encouraged, grow. I began to see the fullness come out of him. We weren't and are not perfect; we are two different people, with two ideas, occupying the same space, yet we love God mutually. Above all, we both made a decision that we were willing to make it work. When he proposed to me, he did not even have a ring, one, because he did not know that he was going to propose to me the day that he did and secondly, because he had not acquired the money to buy what he felt I needed. But clearly, he felt like the moment *was* right. We were having a simple conversation and he just popped the question. I was taken aback because it was so unexpected. We were both coming out of debt, cleaning it up, in fact, so a ring was not my priority, really. Our wedding was small and intimate because a wedding was not what was most important; that is a day versus the rest of our lives. I did not want to be in debt in order to try to prove anything to anyone.

When we met, my ministry was already up and running. When we became serious and then married, I wondered how it was all going to work. Early in our relationship, he came to me and said that God had told him that he was not sending him to take over anything. He said, "I was sent to bring to you whatever you were missing and to support whatever you have." For me, that was a phenomenal statement. What I have come to appreciate the most about my husband is that I have never had to be less of who I am to make him feel like more of who he is. That he has strength enough to let me be strong, and at the same time, when I need to be vulnerable, I can be that. He is the answer to my prayers wrapped in flesh.

Dr. Nikita C. Garris-Watson

Knowing Who You Are

"If most of us remain ignorant of ourselves, it is because self-knowledge is painful and we prefer the pleasures of illusion" (Aldous Huxley).

In my first marriage, I wanted my husband to complete me and make me feel a beautiful, confident and wanted. When you allow a person to build you up, you also give them permission to bring you down. I had to be whole the second time around. As much as I love James, he doesn't complete me; he compliments me. He can comfort me, but he can't complete me.

I learned what it meant to put your heart in the hands of God. How to rest in God – how to genuinely relax. I have always enjoyed my own space, but I had now found a sense of tranquility, not because I was running from anybody or anything. It was because I wanted to be in God's presence. I was really glad that God allowed me the privilege of getting to know Him intimately, and in getting to know God, I got to know myself. I got to appreciate some things about myself. I still had flaws that I wanted to fix, but God taught me to be able to appreciate who I was. So I had to know me in order to know what I wanted.

In the time between relationships, I remember when I was crying out to God one day about my future – about relationships and other things I wanted to see happen – and God said, "You know how to tell me what you want, but you haven't told me what you *don't* want." I was floored; did it really matter to God that in my personal life there were things that I didn't want? God literally compelled me to write a list of not just what I *wanted* (because He can give you that and it still may possess what you don't want), but also what I *didn't* want. I had to articulate for Him both what I needed and wanted, and then did not want. Then I had to look at both lists to see if they were realistic, measurable, or was I asking for something that I could or could not give. It made me examine what was important to me. Writing the list required me to examine my heart and any hidden issues that may have still resided there.

As I embarked upon the relationship and subsequent marriage with James, one of the first things that I requested of him was not to buy me anything. He had to give me him, not things; things are not important to me. Most people look at me and assume that I am high maintenance, but I am really low key. I'm not into a whole lot of stuff. I had learned this about me several years before meeting him, and was completely okay with it. I needed my husband's heart, and not what came from his hands. I told him that I'd rather struggle *with* him than to live my life without him. I needed for my husband to be a prayer warrior – to have a heart for God. That was important! I really wanted a man of God.

Let me point out that there is nothing wrong with liking nice things and pursuing the goal of acquiring items altogether, but when getting *things*, they can become a burden and not a blessing. If a person is left feeling inadequate because of what they can't buy from the store, it simply is not worth. Likewise, having grown up with so little and losing so much each time we moved, I simply never developed an attachment to materials. However, like many others, I enjoy a pretty present in a box every once in a while, but if the present is going to deny me my husband's physical presence, I say, "keep it."

By the same token, I needed for my husband to be strong because I have seen so many men compromise on being who they are. As a female pastor, I asked God for a strong male presence in the church – an elder – so that people would have balance in what they saw. People see strong women all of the time, but I felt that they needed to see a consistent, integrally strong man as well. When I prayed for the strong man for the ministry, I didn't know that the strong man would be my husband. I am a strong person and I am very passionate about my ideas; I needed someone who could handle that and not take it as a personal attack on his importance in my life and relevance in the overall scheme of things.

My husband and I have what we call 'Rough, Rugged and Raw' conversations, and I love them because in those exchanges, we can say whatever is on our heart and mind without having to filter it. It might be the craziest thing, but we can say it without the fear of hearing about it again later in a different conversation! Now, these conversations are open to any topic whether it is something that has happened with us or something that we have had to tackle. The thoughts might come out randomly and might not make sense, but there is the freedom of release that we share in these moments that draws us closer to one another. I have learned about some of my husband's deepest fears and greatest dreams because these moments were safe. That's what I appreciate. Likewise, knowing my own mind, I am not easily swayed by someone else's ideas. James was able to see my passionate pursuit and accept that even in my strong-willed approach to life, it did not stop me from appreciating his thoughts, ideas and leadership.

Take the concept of submission, for example. I'm as strong as they come, but I know how to submit; unfortunately, the perception of submission has been tainted. It is not the loss of my voice, or my opinion. The *Bible* speaks not just of a wife's submission to her husband, but also of the mutual submission of husband and wife to each other (Ephesians 5:21). What I have learned is that submission is a matter of trust and those who struggle with issues of trust that they have harbored for a long time or issues of trust with the person that they are in a relationship with, experience the greatest level of difficulty with it. In marriage, there has to be a confidence that the other person has your best interest at heart. When I came into my second marriage, the good thing was that James also had his own relationship with God; he knew what was important for him. We would have to work to find out what mattered the most to each of us individually and what was up for compromise. For example, for him, taking out the trash and taking care of the cars is important. Despite my independence, I was glad to relinquish these roles because I don't want to take out the trash and not having to pump gas has become a treat for me. ☺

There's this assumption that strength is synonymous with aggression. That is not the case because strength can be silent, it can be unspoken; my greatest strength is being able to lie on my face and talk to God about things. In knowing myself, I gained the ability to not be in conflict with others, and especially my husband. He and I really are stronger together. When we minister, we both understand that it doesn't matter who's in the pulpit because both of us are prepared to back the other person up.

One of my greatest experiences with my husband was when we first started dating, he had never seen deliverance and rarely heard speaking in tongues; he came from a more traditional religious background, so it was foreign to him. The first time he came to hear me preach, he witnessed deliverance and tongues with his own eyes; he was standing in the front pew in amazement, maybe even more so because the event included males and females. I just knew our relationship was over as I looked over at him. But when I got tired during the movement of the spirit and preaching, as if by spiritual instinct, he came and stood behind me praying and watching over me as I finished working the altar.

That's how we flow even now. When one is tired, the other person steps in.

The first time I married, the flesh chose. The second time, God chose for me, and that makes a difference. This is not to say that God cannot perfect something we choose for ourselves, but it's something different when God chooses for you. He understands what you need. We've been married now for five years, and in those years, we have had to learn much about one another. We've had to understand the needs, the ebbs and the flows of the other; when you are older and have spent time in the face of God, you come into a relationship with a whole different mindset. We are more willing to find the place of compromise because we love each other.

Dr. Nikita C. Garris-Watson

Love, Leadership and Legacy

"... because of your partnership in the gospel from the first day until now"
(Philippians 1:5 NIV).

Controversy did not end with my accepting my call to preach, walking in the role of pastor, nor marrying my husband. If anything else, it brought with it a greater series of challenges to be faced. James and I, ourselves, went to God about our marriage. We fasted and we prayed before we got married. He gave us one very clear warning: "Don't put your relationship before me." We have purposed ourselves to keep God first: to keep God in the center.

There are some things that people will try to pigeon-hole you in, and it is based on their misguided opinions of scripture or even on their own personal prejudices. There are people who say that because my husband and I are divorced and remarried, we are going to hell. There was another group of people in the beginning who questioned whether or not we should be married because I was a pastor or whether God would even bless the union. Having spent too much of my walk trying to defend my call against those who take issue with women in ministry, I found encountering these people to be wasted energy that I could not afford to expend.

Because we came into this marriage with two children each of our own, we never looked for "The Brady Bunch" experience; what we wanted was that we could love our children and our children could still love both sets of parents and there not be conflict. People wanted conflict and we would refuse to participate in it.

We made a decision early on that we were married to one another, and the outside opinions had little to no value in our life. And that's not out of arrogance; that's from knowing that you have to protect what is important.

One of the greatest deliberations among outsiders included the fact that having already founded a church when I met my husband, I would be in the role of Senior Pastor - Senior Servant as I prefer to call it - both before and after our marriage. The issue would become a problem for others, but not for us because we had talked about the roles we would play in our relationship before we got married. Six o'clock AM prayer together was our first joint endeavor prior to marriage and we spent time listening to the voice of God not for what we wanted to hear, but for what God required of us. Having heard God clearly, individually and collectively together, we decided to proceed with ministry as a team.

We would be directly challenged about what we heard, but had to make the choice to not allow outside opinions to change our outlook or direction. This was not to encourage being unteachable or even being unwilling to hear alternate views as we have strong wisdom counsel that we seek with consistency, but there are moments when others won't be able to understand what God has spoken to you about *you*. Ultimately, it is the personal relationship with God that matters most. This is where you have to place yourself before God and allow Him to guide you.

There couldn't be two people who more externally different and yet, internally, are so much alike. My husband is an extrovert and I'm an introvert. He doesn't meet a stranger; I am more reserved with strangers. We are SO different, but because of that, we work well together. I tell people that because we are so different, we have a 360 degree view on the world, especially on the adversary. Because we don't see things the same way, I can ask what he sees and vice versa. My husband is a visionary; he is not an administrator. I am; execution is what I do. So because we know our roles, we flow at moments effortlessly. It is the appreciation for what makes us different that God uses for His glory.

What I appreciate most about James is that he has demonstrated through word and action the utmost respect for me as a minister and leader. We've gone to places where people will speak to him and not to me, and he's stopped the conversation to include me and inform them. Where it would be easier to let disrespect slide, my husband has stood boldly to defend his belief not just in me, but in others to those who possess speculative bias. Everyone is entitled to their personal preferences, but we refuse to allow this to become our personal problems.

When you deal with people and their varying opinions, there are those whose self-appointed purpose in life is to look for issues where there are none. They try to look for conflict where there is no conflict. I am not the type of leader that has to be referred to by a title. It is so unimportant to me. I am a Senior Servant and that is how I see myself, and my husband and I both have hearts of service. He is the intercessor of intercessors. I call him Enoch because he and God talk all of the time, even in his sleep. So as long as God is pleased and James and I are comfortable with our roles and positions, we are really not worried about the rest of the world being approving. Seeking the approval of the masses will only lead to mess. We do not argue theology as people want us to. Our unified voice is "Check our fruit." As long as we have fruit, meaning people being built up, being better for being a part of the ministry and demonstrating the principles of Galatians 5:22, that's all that matters to us.

I was made in the image of God (Genesis 1:27). I don't have a question about who I am; I've never wanted to be a man. I like men, I love my man, but I don't want to be *like* any man. I'm just trying to be all that God has called me to be, and my husband supports that. If we allow the world or worldly opinions to get into our relationship, then it's going to become an obstacle. But we don't. We don't give the world access like that. People have opinions, but we found that we have outlived those opinions. Opinions have the potential to obstruct and oppress if given the wrong weight in our lives. They differ to the point of being divisive, and the enemy likes to use division, especially in marriage, to bring on destruction. We don't do that because we get down in the grit together.

Our marriage has not been without struggle, however, because rebuilding from our past while at the same time building up a ministry is a challenge. For those who understand being a "church plant," when you are building a church from the ground up, it can cost you everything. After facing great hurdles and faith battles, at one point, we had a moment where we had both decided that we were going to walk away from ministry and just go and "do us." We had counted our spiritual, personal and financial costs and decided that it was not worth the toll to continue. That didn't work, for it was not the will of God concerning our lives or destinies. The scripture declares in 1 Samuel 15:22 that obedience is better than sacrifice, but we found obedience to be a sacrifice. We are doing this – are in this – together. We don't feel that bondage. If you allow people to, they will put you in religious bondage. What my husband and I have is a *relationship*.

Chapter 13 ~ My One Constant

"We increase our ability, stability and responsibility, when we increase our sense of accountability to God" (Unknown).

Throughout it all, my grandmother and her faith has been and still is a constant in my life. I've seen this woman go through things that other people wouldn't understand and she still would say, "God knows about that, too." I learned how to pray from my grandmother. She may not have the academic accolades, but she has a faith degree that people will never be able to take away from her. My grandmother opens up the door every morning to give thanks. She told me once that "No matter if it's raining, snowing or sunny, I still give thanks to God for this day because I can see it." She still sits in her chair every day and prays for everyone in the family. I am tickled when I go to the house to check on her and she petitions to be prayed for. Whether her body is hurting or not, she stands up in honor of God. When you are done praying for her, she turns around and without fail prays for you.

Her example of faith often challenged me at the moments I wanted to accept failure. For example, when I was in basic training at Fort Jackson, South Carolina, and my body was just worn out near the end, I called her and said, "Grandma, I'm tired. I don't want to do this anymore."

"You are not and have never been a quitter," she responded. She only spoke nine words, but I heard so much more resonate inside of me. I heard what she said and even what she didn't.

I have forever, since that moment, held onto those words because if my grandmother said those words, then she was seeing something in me that I was trying to see in myself. Even with the tough experiences I had in undergraduate school, I could not quit. I remember on graduation day, the skies opened and torrential rain came down. I was soaking wet from it and had decided that I was not going to bother walking across the stage to graduate. They sent us to the gym and when I got there, my grandmother was coming in the door; she was soaking wet. Had I not seen her, I would have walked out. I thought that if she were willing to come and see me graduate in the rain, and get that wet, then I needed to stay. And I did.

Visits with my grandmother are *always* a mood lifter. When I go and her see, she makes me, and anyone who visits her, feel like they are the best person in the world, as though royalty has come to visit. She thanks you for coming to see her; she tells you how much she has missed you. There is this affirmation and love that you receive from her. That's why she's my constant.

I am ashamed to say, though, that I was not always there for her when she needed me. When my grandfather died, I withdrew from her because I thought that she was going to go next. They had been married for over 50 years as I've mentioned before; he was her first and only love and the father of all of her children. You hear stories of how couples who have spent their entire lives together and when one dies, the other soon follows. That's what I thought was going to happen to her, not knowing how resilient this woman truly was. So for a couple of years, I did not fully engage with her. I did not go and see her as often. It was as if I was already mourning the loss of her, but she wasn't yet gone. God had to show me this one day. I was literally mourning for someone who was still here. That was a wake-up call for me, and so I had to go and see her to reconnect and re-engage with her.

My grandmother is still *the* constant in my life. I can call her today and it will be as if time has not passed since we last saw one another. Her house is what I consider to be home. She has lived there all of my life – again, for over 60 years. For a person who has had nothing but instability, to have someone who is there, stable, makes such a huge difference. Just driving onto her street gives me a sense of peace; she's there and the house is there. I've come to rely on that constancy, maybe a little too much.

I remember an incident when I was living with her; she was always there when I came home from high school, which was new for me because, again, I had been a latchkey kid all of my life. Anyway, my grandfather (he was still alive then) had a television repair shop in the basement and she worked down there with him. She would come upstairs when I came in; dinner would be on the table at six o'clock every day except for Saturdays.

On this particular day when I came home, she was nowhere to be found; neither was my grandfather. I had become accustomed to her being there, and started walking around the house looking for her. The house was dark; not even the kitchen light was on that would normally not be turned off until my grandfather had settled in for the night. When I could not find her or my grandfather, I thought the "rapture" had happened. 'The Lord had come and taken her up to heaven with Him.' I was done! This was pre-cell phone days, so I had no one to call to check and see if she was with them. I was FRANTIC!

Now, other people were around in the neighborhood, but in my silly mind, I thought maybe they were all going to hell with me because she wasn't there. My grandmother had a set routine; it was not the day for her to go and get her hair done. It wasn't

Saturday, her grocery store day. It was a random Tuesday and she was supposed to be home. So I was **CONVINCED** that the rapture had already come and I had been left behind.

When she finally walked through the door, I was weeping. I ran to her and just held on tight. She thought I had lost my mind.

"What's wrong with you, child?" I told her what I thought had happened. She was so tickled and turned red in the face laughing so much. She said something like, "Baby!"

Y'all, I thought I had missed Jesus. I was not ready for that. You can all stop laughing now. ☺

Chapter 14 ~ Lessons I've Learned

"Life's best lessons seem to be learned at the worst times" (Unknown).

Life would teach me hard lessons, but God would turn the hurt into hope and help. I believe of all that I have learned, faith and trust presented the greatest challenges. The thing about both of these is that they are not a constant, but rather a continuous process that is only cultivated when put into practice. While the scripture points out in Matthew 17:20, "if you [have] faith even as small as a mustard seed, you could say to this mountain, 'Move from here to there,' and it would move," Nothing would be impossible," I would learn that a mustard seed was the minimum and that the mountains would only get larger. God had a plan for my life and my past was only going to be an acceptable excuse for a period.

In learning to trust God, I had to learn how to willing get over the "Daddy Damage." I had a difficult time of seeing God as Father – Abba. This was a process because I had to detox from the damage and permit God to download into me new insight. I had never fully understood what the impact of an absent father and abusive father figures could do to me internally. I didn't realize how I had entered God's presence with apprehension fully expecting to be rejected by Him at any moment. I didn't know that I was convinced that the love of God had limits and that I was waiting to be punished versus protected. I couldn't conceive that God was not setting me up for failure and public humiliation. Deep down, internally, I was not fully convinced that God loved me.

Dr. Nikita C. Garris-Watson

The awesome thing I would learn is that the God who created me and called me was not willing to easily give up on me. He was not intimidated by my questions and could handle His own when it came to my inquiries. He had a plan, and purging me of this pain was part of the process.

In learning to trust God, I began to allow Him to strategically place people in my life. I've learned the importance of relationships, and again, how to trust because it is still an issue for me. But in learning how to trust, it also allowed God to heal the broken places and show me who He had placed in my life. I could no longer live as a loner avoiding people in an effort to avoid pain with everything in me. I've always tried to be kind to people, but I kept them at a distance not allowing access to anything but the most shallow parts of me; like a solider caught by the enemy, I was only willing to share my name, rank and serial number and that was it, but every person that I was to meet was not the enemy. That did not mean that every relationship was perfect, or that every relationship turned out the way I wanted it to. And so what I found out was how to hold on to the ones that are good and let the others go without harboring the bitterness with which I was so familiar.

I would find that some people wanted more from me than what I could or would give. I would be strengthened not to be apologetic about having boundaries and protecting me. I am still a very private person. I am still protective of me, but not so much to where nobody can get in.
Relationships still take work for me, but I do have some pretty great people in my life. He has ordained friends and relationships in my life that I did not seek out, and yet they formed in ways that did not make sense to me then or even now. And what I like about those people is that they are ordained by God to be able to handle my

moments of needing to be quiet. They can handle that I can't be on the phone every day.

Growing up so fast and intensely, I'm still by nature very serious. I have moments where I can sit and laugh, but on the whole, I am a very serious person, and they can appreciate that. I try to be there for other people as much as possible. I try to be the friend that I want to be while understanding the limitations.

Briefly going back to the discussion of living in a silo, I also mean that there were those moments where I felt like it was just me and God against the world. God had to show me that I really wasn't alone as much as I thought I was. So, I wouldn't say that my overprotectiveness is gone; I just control it better now. There are still certain situations or moments where I will put up my guard, which can be positive sometimes because I've needed to put that guard up. I have learned to trust my spirit and not what my natural eye sees. It helps me to see beyond people's behaviors sometimes and into their brokenness or spirits.

I've also learned how not to internalize things. There were times when I would overthink so badly, I'd get headaches because I was analyzing things too hard. I was guilty of analysis-paralysis. I would overanalyze or try to fix or figure out why things happen or what was wrong. I always looked at it from the viewpoint of what was wrong with me, and I had to learn that that was not always the case. It was not always something wrong with me.

I can't say this enough, but I had to learn how to trust God, and that was after learning how to see Him as God and how to trust Him as Savior and to trust Him from the Abba-Father perspective. I had to trust that He really was a Jeremiah 29:11 God: He did not intend evil for my life. So when people ask me questions like, 'What do you do when you go through hell?' or 'Why would God allow bad things to happen?' I don't think it is so much as an "allowing," but rather it's our individual choices. We all have free will, and we can become victims of the free will of others.

I remember one day I was sitting in my office, and I was crying out to God. I was asking Him to help me with this or that. God said what I thought was the strangest thing. He said in my spirit, "You are obedient, but you have no faith. You will do anything I tell you to do, but you are not willing to really ask me for anything that is not in your power to do nor do you trust me beyond the moment." I did not realize until that then that I had stopped dreaming. I'd stopped hoping. Anything that required me to stretch beyond what I could see, I wasn't doing. I'd stopped planning. I had arrived at the place where I was not willing to expect anything, thus, I could not be disappointed. It was so much a part of me that I had not recognized that it was in conflict with what I was saying that I believed about God.

If God had told me to run around the building four times, I'd do it, but there was no expectation on my part after that run. So I was obedient, but I had no faith. He had to take me through a faith process, and, admittedly, that was the scariest thing to me. There are two things I've battled all my life: the spirit of fear and the spirit of the unknown. I don't do well with not knowing what is going to happen; I need to know what I am up against. So there were moments where I had to plant my feet and my faith, and just deal with the unknown. No figuring out, no planning it out. I just had to walk it out. I was being moved from theology (knowing scriptures) to walk-ology (having to walk the scriptures out); belief had to become behavior before I could see the next level of what God had in store for me.

Undoubtedly, evil is present. I went through hell when I didn't have God in my life. If I am going to go through hell now, at least I have the comfort of knowing that He is there with me. God is looking out for me and still requires much of me. I am a realist, not an idealist. I expect that life is going to happen. We are going to have issues and challenges; everything will not always be wonderful. The word warns us that "man who is born of a woman is few of days and full of trouble" (John 14:1). Because I see things in black and white already, I expect that there are going to be moments of trouble, yet I've learned how not to get stuck in those moments. I see them for what they are. The places where I used to get stuck, I don't anymore. I don't get consumed to where I cannot function. That's a lesson I had to learn. I had to learn how to walk by faith and not by sight.

I've survived. That's what my ministry has become a symbol of – the transparency of it all. If my story, my past, can save someone from experiencing the same pain, then I have to take the risk, and sharing my story is risk for me. But I must be obedient to God even when it doesn't make sense to me. It's another moment for me where obedience is better than sacrifice, but yet, in this case, obedience *is* sacrifice because I'm sacrificing my privacy. It is the first lesson of having that trust in God that has allowed me to do this. I have to trust that it is all going to work together for my good.

Dr. Nikita C. Garris-Watson

Do What!!

Dr. Nikita C. Garris-Watson

Final Words from Pastor Ki

"To live is to suffer, to survive is to find some meaning in the suffering" (Friedrich Nietzsche).

As I face the fact that my most intimate pain and private deliverance is now subject to public scrutiny and passionate dialogue, *how* I wish this book had the ability to solve all of the problems for those who have read its pages or somehow remove the pain of what has been experienced, whether at the hands of others or oneself. But that is neither the case nor the cause for my being obedient in sharing a portion of my story. Instead, what I truly pray is that as you have followed the ebbs and flow of my journey that you have found the possibilities that lie beneath your problems. According to Webster's Dictionary, damaged, by definition, is "to inflict physical harm on (something) so as to impair its value, usefulness, or normal function," whereas, destined is "to be directed, devised, or set apart for a specific purpose or place." What I have learned through living and sharing my life's story is that while harm was inflicted with the ultimate intent of lowering my value or usefulness, it had quite the opposite outcome. Yes, for a period in my life, I did not function "normally," but because I was being directed to a place for a purpose, it was not my dysfunction, but my destiny that would place a demand for my deliverance.

While it took a long time for me to find value in my life or what I had faced, it was God who showed me that He could bring purpose out of pain. God didn't just let me hurt. He let me help. He let what I had gone through help other people. Would I want to relive it all over again? Indeed I would NOT! However, I am willing to be used as an example instead of holding onto any excuses.

Success is often camouflaged in the veil of struggle and I would be doing a great disservice if I didn't make it clear that we have to evolve even when things are still not resolved in our hearts, mind and lives. As I honestly communicated in the introduction, this is not a fairy tale where all things just end well. There are still situations where no apologies have been issued, where denial is the response and avoidance is the answer. There are questions that just have not been answered and doors that simply had to be shut because closure would not come any other way. Decisions determine direction, and had I not made a decision to move forward at the urging of the Holy Spirit, I would still be stuck in those places and crying from the pain inflicted upon me. Thus, I prophetically give to all who need it, permission to move forward and gain healing without carrying the guilt of doing better.

Likewise, everyone won't celebrate your deliverance. Admittedly, it can be disappointing, but it does not have to be a distraction to your destiny. The truth of the matter is that deliverance is a decision followed up by determination. There are too many that simply are not willing to make the decision and lack the determination to see the process through. Some people don't have the capacity to be what you need or want them to be because of their brokenness. Accept their trust, but don't deny your own truth and responsibility to do better for yourself. Don't apologize for deciding that you deserve a better existence. True deliverance does not attempt to make others feel bad, nor stop others from finding freedom. On the contrary, when you are delivered, there is something inside of you that wants it for everyone around you. I decree and declare that you will find the strength to make the decision for your deliverance.

Life will go on and with it, new obstacles will arise; however, these obstacles become opportunities for God to show you a deeper understanding of who He is and a greater appreciation for who you are. I have found that it is because of my life's experiences that I am more humble regarding those who are hurting, more patient with those in pain, more tolerant of those facing turmoil and more loving of those whom others consider lost. I simply don't have the capacity to think arrogantly, for I am too familiar with my own story and how God had to come and rescue me. As they say in the church, "When I look back over my life and all that God has brought me through," one flashback keeps me from falling back. At the same time, I find myself more absolute regarding the ability of God to act on behalf of those who accept Him. I know if He can do it for me, He can certainly do it and more for others.

The enemy will come to test the authenticity of your deliverance, for it is his personal desire to kill, steal and destroy. That is the reason that he has come for so many in the genesis of our lives, for he understood the power that comes from finding out that deliverance is available. One of the greatest weapons of the enemy is to send reminders and ridicule, but I have found God to be a reliable remedy. Let me issue this clarification; the altar is absolutely the place where we are altered before God, but it is not to be viewed as the only answer to our needs. I am a strong proponent, where needed, of getting licensed psychological counseling in conjunction with strong spiritual guidance. The two-part combination has the ability to provide a more effective healing approach.

Instead of looking for perfection, celebrate your progress; each of us is a work in progress. I have found that detours are a part of the road to destiny. Not all detours are demonic in nature; there are times when the course has to be changed. One of the greatest challenges can be trying to understand the purpose of the detour, but having served God, I have come to realize that He is never caught off guard; in fact, it was He who ordained the detour that allowed me to bypass what would have been a hindrance to my destiny. As I learned to follow my spiritual GPS, I would find myself further up the road and sooner than expected because I was learning to trust God who was guiding me.

Once you come out, stay out, but if you fall short, come back out. Don't allow the enemy to hold you hostage. Persistent pursuit of purpose can have pitfalls along the way. There are still moments when I have to deal with my natural versus my spiritual responses to matters. The goal is not to be condemned, but to be convicted to change. We all have to reach a place where we confront what we want to change, otherwise, it is simply complaining. There is no guarantee that it will be easy, but it certainly is possible. It should be noted that few things change overnight and even fewer all at once. What I have learned is that as I was growing in one area, I found it less stressful to face other areas of my life. There were moments that I felt I was losing me, but I found a better me in the end.

Ultimately, I pray that whether I have had the pleasure of meeting each of you, Dear Reader, personally or not, that something was read which helped to heal a private place of pain. Perhaps my story is not your story, but reading this will help you to help someone else to find hope and healing. Just know that I purposed myself to pray over the life of every reader that God would get the glory out of your story.

And if you have not yet had the chance to meet my Savior, let me take this moment to introduce you. Saying the Sinner's Prayer is declaring to God that you are relying on Jesus Christ as your Savior. It is faith in Jesus' death and resurrection that saves us.

The ABCs of Salvation

A—ADMIT Admit to God that you are a sinner (Romans 3:10, 23; Romans 6:23). Repent, turning away from your sin (Acts 3:19; 1 John 1:9).
B—BELIEVE Believe that Jesus is God's Son and accept God's gift of forgiveness from sin (Romans 5:8; Acts 4:12; John 1:2; John 3:16; John 14:6; Ephesians 2:8-9; John 1:11-13).
C—CONFESS Confess your faith in Jesus Christ as Savior and Lord (Romans 10:9-10, 13).

Sinner's Prayer

Father, I understand that I am a sinner and I ask You for forgiveness. I believe that your son, Jesus Christ, died on the cross for my sins so that I could receive Your forgiveness and have eternal life. I ask Jesus to come into my life right now and become my personal Savior. From this day forward, Lord, I give You control of my life to rule and reign in my heart. Make me a new person and help me to live for You. In Jesus' name I pray, Amen.

If this is your first time, I welcome you to the Kingdom family, and if you are returning to your faith, I welcome you back home. I encourage you not to try and do it alone, but find a church home where you feel comfortable and continue your journey with God.

Prayer of Deliverance

To you, Dear Reader. As I have thought about you in my heart, this is a snippet of the prayer that I prayed for you.

Dr. Nikita C. Garris-Watson

Father God in the name of Jesus, Yyou said in Your word to cast our cares upon You because You care for us and Lord, I cast up to You every person who has been chosen to read ***Damaged, but Destined*** knowing that this is the work You have called me to do. I pray, Father, that they will find the strength to come boldly to the throne of grace to obtain Your mercy in their time of need (Hebrews 4:16). Help them, Lord, to repent of all sins both known and unknown that have kept them from the fullness of life with You. Father, I pray that as they read this book, that You have begun delivering them from the enemies that are too strong for them to handle on their own (Psalm 18:17). Lord, lead them and guide them continually, for Your namesake (Psalm 31:3; John 16:13). Make the crooked places straight and the rough places smooth that they may find You (Isaiah 40:4).

Lord, I plead the blood over their past and seal all access points of the enemy. Father, break the hold of every excruciating experience, miserable memory, abuse inflicted, act of violation or violence, negative words spoken, hidden secrets kept and painful punishments endured. Tear down and curse at the root every spirit of unforgiveness, bitterness, anger, resentment, envy, strife, rejection, self-hate, insecurity, inferiority, self-pity, depression, shame, guilt, pride, frustration, rebellion, stubbornness, hatred, fear and every other stronghold that has held them bound (2 Corinthians 10:4). Father, create in them a clean heart and renew a right spirit within them (Psalm 51:10). Loose to them the spirit of power, love and a sound mind (2 Timothy 1:7). Lord, set them free and help them to live free indeed (John 8:36).

Lord, give them power to resist the enemy (James 4:7) and let not the enemy kill, steal or destroy their destiny (John 10:10). Father, I ask that You would give them strength to bring forth destiny (Isaiah 66:9) despite the damage that life has done. In the name of Jesus, I pray and believe it to be so. Amen!

Beloved, know that I am praying for and with you always.

Kingdom Blessings and Hugs wrapped in the love of God!

Dr. Ki

Dr. Nikita C. Garris-Watson

ABOUT THE AUTHOR

Dr. Nikita C. Garris-Watson, the "Stiletto Preacher," is a humble and willing servant of the Lord and His people. A survivor of childhood and adult physical, sexual and emotional abuse, she has chosen to use the painful tests, trials and tribulations of her life, not as excuses for failure, but rather as battle axes and weapons of war to bring Deliverance to the Neighborhood and the Nations.

A licensed and ordained minister of the Gospel, Dr. Garris-Watson has been blessed by strong ministerial training and leadership affording her the opportunities to serve the body of Christ as an intercessor, evangelist, prophet, bible teacher, praise team member, associate minister and conference preacher. Professionally, she is the director of a college preparatory program and an adjunct professor. Dr. Garris-Watson views wisdom as a gift from God and, thus, has earned a Bachelor's, two Master's degrees and a Doctorate of Ministry along with other post-graduate work. Dr. Garris-Watson has served as the guest host of her own radio segment called "Inspirational Moments with Dr. Ki."

Dr. Garris-Watson, or "Dr. Ki" as she is affectionately known, is the Founder and Senior Pastor of Words of Deliverance Worldwide Ministries and Executive Director of HerStory Ministries. Anointed excellence is her personal standard and her heartfelt prayer is to be used of God to bring about spiritual deliverance, destroy generational curses, eradicate spiritual paralysis, evoke healing and birth permanent change in the lives of God's people. It is to this effort that she is preparing to release two books and a clothing line using the profits as the foundation for funding a major community outreach effort geared towards the underrepresented members of our society.

Dr. Ki is married to "the answers to her prayers wrapped in flesh," the Bishop-Elect James E. Watson, Executive Pastor of WODWM, and together, they share two sons and two daughters. Although striving to greatly impact the Kingdom, they share the belief that family is a ministry like none other and should be protected at all cost.

<u>Social Media Information:</u>
Website: www.WODWM.org
Twitter: www.twitter.com/DrNCGW
Facebook: www.facebook.com/DrNCGW
Periscope: www.periscope.com/DrNCGW

COMING SOON*!*

DAMAGED BUT DESTINED: SO WHAT? NOW WHAT! – STUDY GUIDE

DAMAGED BUT DESTINED: DELIVERANCE DIARY – PROVOKED BY THE PROVERBS